"Lenny Luchetti has provided a new approach to an old problem, but one not frequently associated with preaching. That is the problem—and necessity—of empathy in the pulpit. Luchetti gives to preachers a practical and theological framework against which we may measure our preaching, our ministry, and our own hearts. This is a valuable book for us all."

—**Richard Lischer**, James T. and Alice Mead Cleland Professor Emeritus of Preaching, Duke Divinity School, Durham, NC; author, *The End of Words* and *Stations of the Heart*

"Do not read the title and think this is only for preachers. Empathy has become a lost ingredient of our culture, and this book speaks to what has been lost. In addition, the science, theology, sociology, and biblical depth of the subject of empathy is explored. This phrase jumped off the page to me: 'We are wired for empathy created in God's Image'—powerful words of hope. At the same time, Dr. Luchetti gives practical and specific methods in which a preacher may increase empathy by drawing upon models of the past and current exercises. This book should be at the top of one's reading list and, of course, especially for preachers. Compelling and inspiring for times like these!"

—**Jo Anne Lyon,** ambassador, General Superintendent, Emerita, The Wesleyan Church, Indianapolis, IN

To Dr. Wright,
An empathic leader who inspires me to love God and people more.
— Lenny Luchetti

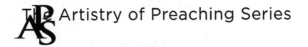

The Artistry of Preaching Series

Preaching with Empathy
Crafting Sermons in a Callous Culture

Lenny Luchetti

Abingdon Press™
Nashville

PREACHING WITH EMPATHY:
CRAFTING SERMONS IN A CALLOUS CULTURE

Copyright © 2018 by Abingdon Press

All rights reserved.

This book is printed on acid-free paper.

Library of Congress Cataloging-in-Publication Data has been requested.

ISBN 978-1-5018-4172-9

18 19 20 21 22 23 24 25 26 27—10 9 8 7 6 5 4 3 2 1
MANUFACTURED IN THE UNITED STATES OF AMERICA

Contents

Series Preface

The Artistry of Preaching series gives practical guidance on matters that receive insufficient attention in preaching literature yet are key for preachers who seek greater creative expression in their preaching. Fresh, faithful proclamation requires imagination and creative engagement of the Bible and our world. There is no shortage of commentaries on the Bible and books on biblical interpretation for preaching, but there is a shortage of practical resources to help strengthen the creativity of preachers to facilitate their proclamation of the gospel.

The first volume of this series, *Preaching as Poetry: Beauty, Goodness, and Truth in Every Sermon*, redefines preaching for our current postmodern age. The world has changed. Beauty, goodness, and truth no longer mean what they used to mean as fixed absolute and universal standards. While this may be threatening to some preachers, the new meanings can actually allow preachers fresh and creative ways to proclaim God's love and saving purposes in a rapidly changing world. Preaching needs to be reconceived as a kind of poetry, in the sense of communicating the wondrous beauty of God's saving purposes and promises in troubled times. God needs to be presented in terms of experience and relationships, more than abstractions, and faith needs to be presented as something that adds beauty, goodness, and truth to life. In other words, for a new generation that seeks concrete outcomes and immediate benefits, faith needs to be presented as a relationship with God and neighbor that affords deep meaning and great joy.

The second volume of the series, *Actuality: Real-Life Stories for Sermons That Matter*, by Scott Hoezee, is a resource for preachers who want guidance to be better storytellers or to use story more effectively to communicate with a new generation. There readers will also find a collection of stories that both preach and stimulate their imaginations to identify stories from their own contexts. Preachers can easily run out of good stories to use that embody the gospel. The problem is not a shortage of stories; they are all around in everyday events. The task is learning how to harvest them, as will be shown here. Preachers long for good stories, and today's listeners are not content with the canned internet illustrations that sound artificial and have a predictable moral. Rather they want stories rooted in the actual world in which they live, that depict life as they know it, and that can function as Jesus's stories did, as parables and metaphors that bear God's grace to their hearers.

The third volume, *Preaching in Pictures: Using Images for Sermons that Connect*, helps preachers add some spark and imagination with a dominant or captivating image. The challenge is not just to find images that are visually evocative; it is to find ones that are artistic, propulsive, and theologically centered. By moving from a theme sentence to an image statement, preachers can move their composition from being a "beautiful mess" to an affective sermon. Preachers can benefit from the book's practical exercises adapted from creative writers and poets that help in the art of selecting images and polishing them for use in relation to biblical texts. Equally important in the current times, readers will find guidance on using images on screens in worship that can powerfully assist the work of the Spirit and increase the joy of preaching.

This fourth volume of The Artistry of Preaching series is *Preaching with Empathy: Crafting Sermons in a Callous Culture* by Lenny Luchetti. Empathy is a subject that some people might not connect with art and artistry. They may think of empathy as a feature of personality, something one either has or does not have. To some degree, they are right. What makes the present volume so remarkable is that Lenny Luchetti teaches the art of putting empathy into practice in preaching. However great or small our natural empathy, it can be enhanced by tending to it.

Empathy is needed for preaching to be transformative for the listeners and society in general. It is not enough for preachers just to know they love their congregations. The congregations must know it. Preachers must show it, ensuring that it is experienced through what is done and said. Empathy must be nurtured and communicated through what one says about the Bible and the world today, and about the various relationships fostered in preaching. While the preacher's love for the people is essential, the goal of empathic homiletical practice is to communicate God's love in Christ and through the Spirit, to enable the people's ministry, through empathy for one another. In other words, empathy is a spiritual practice that individual preachers can cultivate and utilize to enhance their sermons, as Luchetti shows and as many have done through history. His volume could not come at a better time, when so much in the current culture seems to point toward apathy. He brings a corrective that is hopeful, practical, encouraging, and inspiring.

The aim of the series is to be practical, to provide concrete guidelines and exercises for preachers to follow, and to assist them in engaging practices. Preaching is much more than art, yet by ensuring that we as preachers employ artistry in our preaching, we assist the Holy Spirit in communicating the gospel to a new generation of people seeking God.

—Paul Scott Wilson, Series Editor

Acknowledgments

Countless professors, authors, students, pastors, and congregants have shaped my preaching practice. They, like the Artistry of Preaching series, have taught me the value of merging theological substance with practical relevance. If this book adds value to your ministry, they get the credit. If it doesn't, I'll take the blame.

Paul Scott Wilson has been a constant source of encouragement and refinement during this project. He cares deeply about preaching, as evidenced by his long tenure and excellence as a professor and author in the field of homiletics. *Preaching with Empathy* is better because of his gentle guidance.

Constance Stella and the Abingdon Press team are passionate—persistent even—about putting smart practical resources in the hands of church leaders. I applaud Abingdon's commitment to develop tools that help us thoughtfully navigate the complexities of ministry today.

Several friends and colleagues expended the time, energy, and expertise to read portions of my work and offer constructive commendation and critique. Bud Bence, John Drury, Patrick Eby, Scott Hughes, Safiyah Fosua, Richard Lischer, Aaron Perry, Jason Runyan, Mark Schnell, David Vardaman, and Dave Ward have been wise journey companions on the road to book completion.

Amy, the love of my life, and our three children, Zachary, Liana, and Samuel, fill me with love and laughter. They kept me from taking myself too seriously while I worked on *Preaching with Empathy*, a book I believe has serious implications for the church.

God is the epitome of empathy. In Christ, God empathically entered the hurts and hopes of humanity. *Preaching with Empathy*, the book and the practice, is possible only because we are created in the image of this empathic God. All glory be to God forever and ever. Amen.

Introduction

"Empathy is, in fact, an ideal that has the power both to transform our own lives and to bring about fundamental social change. Empathy can create a revolution."
—Roman Krznaric, *Empathy*

Seminary taught many of us important skills for preaching. We were shown how to exegete a biblical text by probing the literary, historical, and theological contexts. Next in the curricular lineup was the art of rhetoric. Various linear and narrative sermon forms were critiqued or commended. Then we were thrown into a somewhat sterile preaching lab where we tried our best to impress our peers and professor with voice fluctuation, gesture variety, and, of course, eye contact. Seminary professors hoped that students, in the process of learning how to preach, would develop a deep love for God, scripture, and preaching. I suspect most of us did.

There is another love necessary for preaching to reach its full potential for societal transformation—love for those to whom we preach. It's not enough to get the biblical text, sermon form, and delivery right; the preacher must also get the listeners "right." If not, the preacher will "prepare generic sermons for generic humanity that never truly become enfleshed in the real-life situations of particular congregations."[1]

Enter empathy. Empathy gives preachers the capacity, the grace really, to slip their feet into the shoes of their congregants so that they think and feel what their people think and feel. Empathy can make mediocre preaching better, and good preaching great. Without empathy, preachers cannot begin to fully know and love the people to whom they preach. Furthermore, the preacher who lacks empathy will have only a partial view of the God in whose image listeners are made. Empathy that is rooted in and compelled by the trinitarian God has the power to create a revolution in the pulpit and pew that ripples to the ends of the earth.

Simon Baron-Cohen writes, "Empathy itself is the most valuable resource in our world.... Given this assertion, it is puzzling that... it is rarely, if ever, on the agenda."[2] If you feel nobody is listening to, or being transformed by, your preaching, I can relate. Maybe your problem has little to do with exegesis or delivery and a lot to do with empathy.

Love for people drove you into the preaching life, despite its many challenges and risks. A loving connection with the people to whom you deliver the word of life is probably what keeps you preaching when you feel like hanging up the homiletic cleats. Still, at some point along the way, many of us experience an acute case of preaching-exhaustion and people-fatigue. It happened to me about a decade into pastoral ministry.

In the midst of my own exhaustion and limitations, I began to experience a homiletic resurrection. I started, serendipitously, to engage the sermonic process no longer as a rhetorical chore but as a spiritual art that empathically intertwined me with God, people, and the biblical text. I am hopeful that the same resurrection will happen for those who read this book. Is it possible for preachers to practice empathy in ways that enhance their preaching and relationships? That is the goal of this project.

Preaching with Empathy joins together what has too often been torn asunder in order to connect preachers at a more meaningful level with the people in their care. This work brings together an array of interdisciplinary conversation partners, engaging voices from the fields of homiletics, theology, sociology, philosophy, history, and neurology. But this is no theoretical text; it is an unapologetically practical tool for preachers who want to become better people as they preach better sermons.

Preaching with Empathy is for seasoned preachers who want a shot in the arm to heighten their passion for the God they proclaim and the people to whom they make God known. Pastors in the grind of ministry challenges should find much in this volume to immediately employ in their preaching. *Preaching with Empathy* is also written for professors and students of homiletics who are seeking a resource that is theologically thoughtful, discipline-inclusive, and practically useful. I hope that those in the academy find this brief book rich enough in analysis for use in the classroom. The primary audience for this work, then, is thoughtful pastors and seminarians, those who serve in the church and study in the academy.

Think of the book's layout as a house-building adventure. First, the site is prepared by surveying the land. I prepare the site by exploring how cultural apathy (chapter 1), though problematic, actually creates a context that is well suited for homiletic empathy (chapter 2).

Once the site is thoroughly prepared, the foundation is poured. The concrete is a strong mixture of theology, scripture, and history. I situate empathy in a theology of creation, the Trinity, and the incarnation (chapter 3). Then, I throw church history into the mix, exploring the exemplary ways that John Wesley and Martin Luther King Jr. preached with empathy (chapter 4).

When the concrete is set, the rest of the house can be built. It's time to do the framing! While *Preaching with Empathy* has an overtly practical orientation throughout, the framing chapters are especially loaded with practices to foster empathy in preachers and preaching. We start with practical exercises designed to cultivate empathy in preachers (chapter 5). Finally, we consider how to apply empathy directly into the process of developing and delivering sermons (chapter 6). You get to decide, after reading this book, the finishing touches for your homiletic house. Be as creative as you can be when you choose the siding, the paint colors, and the landscaping.

My hope for this book is audacious. When preachers proclaim the gospel with the empathy of Christ flowing into, around, and through their homiletic practices, it will radically transform them and the people to whom they preach. The ripple will reach the community, nation, and world. For God's sake, it must. In a culture that has normalized political hostility, racial tension, domestic violence, and social slander, empathy may be the most potent cure.

There is no guarantee that embracing the perspectives and practices offered in this book will make you a more empathic person. Preaching with empathy is a spiritual art that cannot be reduced to a mechanical technique. I'm convinced, however, that a careful and prayerful reading will increase your empathy and enable you to craft empathic sermons in a callous culture. A preacher who is filled with divine empathy will preach sermons that move heaven and earth. That I *can* guarantee.

I pray that God will multiply the bread and fish of my work so that it becomes more than it ever could be without God. May Christ be incarnated through the sermons of preachers who empathically love God and, with equal passion, human beings made in God's likeness.

Part I: Surveying the Land

Chapter 1
A Culture of Apathy

Apathy Abounds

Apathetic disengagement has become normative in Western society. The human capacity for empathic understanding, feeling, and responding appears to be diminishing. Societal apathy has been mounting for decades and, according to research, is at its peak.

In 1964 at 3 a.m., Kitty Genovese was stabbed to death while returning to her apartment in Queens, New York. According to the *New York Times* journalist covering the story, as many as thirty-eight witnesses saw or heard the attack as it occurred over a thirty-minute span. They did nothing to help the victim. This disturbing event led to the popularizing of the term *bystander apathy* by social psychologists. Allegedly, "Americans became concerned about their lack of concern" after this tragic depiction of apathy at its worst.[1]

Another well-known study, conducted by sociologists at Princeton University in 1973,[2] illustrates the troubling drift toward apathy. Dozens of students training for vocational ministry at Princeton Theological Seminary were the subjects of this study. Some of these students were read the parable of the good Samaritan, told by Jesus in Luke 10:29-37. In this parable, Jesus compared the apathy of a Jewish priest and Levite with the empathy of a Samaritan man. The priest, Levite, and Samaritan took separate journeys along the same road. They each encountered the same person in need of help. Only the Samaritan man possessed the empathy to stop and help the man in need. This empathy, shining brightly compared to the darkness of the priest and Levite's apathetic bypassing, made the Samaritan "good."

The students who heard the parable were sent to another building to give a talk, a sort of mini-sermon, about the parable. Another group of students in the study did not hear the parable and were directed to give a talk on a different topic. As both groups of students journeyed to a building to give their talk, they encountered a man lying on the ground in obvious need of assistance. He was an actor staged in that location. Here's the punch line. Researchers who led the study noted that there was no significant difference between the two groups of students when it came to helping or ignoring the victim. The students who contemplated and prepared to speak about the parable of the good Samaritan were, with a few exceptions, in too much of a hurry to stop and help the person in need of care. "Thinking about the Good Samaritan did not increase helping behavior." In several cases, students who heard the parable literally stepped over the victim to enter the building in which they were giving the talk about the parable.[3]

The Kitty Genovese tragedy and the Princeton experiment hint at the dramatic shift that occurred in the second half of the twentieth century. There were some bright spots of empathy, particularly in the civil rights movement, but societal apathy became, by and large, normalized.

Maybe you're thinking, *That was then, this is now.* Surely contemporary society has progressed from apathy to empathy. Isn't self-preservation less appealing today than it was in 1964, when thirty-eight alleged eye- or ear-witnesses did nothing to help a woman who was attacked and murdered at knifepoint? We have moved beyond the kind of self-absorption revealed in the 1973 Princeton University study, right? Sadly, recent research confirms we still have an empathy shortage and apathy surplus.

Leading up to the 2008 election, presidential candidate Barack Obama lamented the lack of empathy. "There's a lot of talk in this country about the federal deficit. But I think we should talk more about our *empathy deficit*—our ability to put ourselves in someone else's shoes. . . . We live in a culture that discourages empathy, a culture that too often tells us that our principal goal in life is to be rich, thin, young, famous, safe and entertained."[4] It's hard to refute this cultural indictment.

The University of Michigan conducted research in 2010 that showed a significant decline of empathy. "We found the biggest drop in empathy after the year 2000," said Sara Konrath, a researcher at the University of Michigan Institute for Social Research. "College kids today are about forty percent lower in empathy than their counterparts of twenty or thirty years ago, as measured by standard tests of this personality trait." Konrath and her team cite overexposure to media information and violence, the emotional distance of social media, and self-absorption concerning popularity and success as the driving forces behind the findings.[5]

Eminent sociologist Christian Smith corroborates the decline in empathy and the increase in apathy. In his acclaimed book *Souls in Transition*, Smith revealed findings from interviews with thousands of young adults. He tracked their religious beliefs, influences, and practices as they journeyed from eighteen to twenty-four years of age. Smith's study showed that apathy abounds. The majority of young adults believe that helping people is not an obligation but "an optional personal choice," meaning "that nobody has any natural or general responsibility or obligation to help other people."[6]

Apathy can be linked to the sense of fatalism that Smith detected in young adults. "Most emerging adults in America have extremely modest to no expectations for ways society or the world can be changed for the better.... They seem to feel pretty powerless, in some cases hopeless, about influencing the larger public world in which they live."[7] The "why bother" question of yesterday has become the "whatever" exclamation of today. Clearly society has progressed in various ways over the last half century, but there has been a regression of empathy.

Homiletic Apathy

The church is inevitably influenced, for better or worse, by the cultural milieu of the day. Apathy is creeping into the pulpit. There are several causes of homiletic apathy. Doubt about the potential of preaching to transform lives is one of them. To be sure, preachers have always grappled with whether preaching really matters. The struggle, however, is acute today because of the prevalence of voices, even from within the church, that declare preaching has lost its prominence or run its course. Preaching, to some, is a bygone by-product of a different era back when words had weight.

While preachers wonder if preaching really matters, they still expend an average of ten to fifteen hours each week toiling to birth sermons.[8] If preachers develop forty sermons annually, they will devote four hundred to six hundred hours every year to preaching. Many tackle the preaching task while internally engaged in a tug-of-war between the side of them that is hopeful and the side that is doubtful about preaching. As Lori Carrell put it:

> How could words spoken by one person to a relatively small group of people...do any good at all? The challenges are so dreadfully enormous. Indeed, people around the globe share memories of the ravages of recent

years: 9/11, Southeast Asia's tsunami, Hurricane Katrina, Haiti, Japan, the Connecticut school tragedy....These epic tragedies compel universal human ponderings about pain and necessitate a response to suffering, providing both opportunity and overwhelming challenge for those who preach. Perhaps we in the church should not be surprised that this current context creates speculation among preachers about the worth of their endeavors in the pulpit....Does preaching matter?[9]

When doubt surpasses hope, apathy wins. Preachers keep preaching but often with diminished confidence in the homiletic endeavor.

Postmodernity has posed particular challenges to preaching that add fuel to the fire of apathy. Coupled with a sense of fatalism, due in part to broken political promises, widespread terrorism, and economic decline, epistemological skepticism tests the fiber of preaching and preachers. More to the point, we live in a context that is experiencing a pervasive dismissal of the assertion of truth and certainty. As David Lose has said, "The casualty of such skepticism has been certainty, the belief that we can know anything for sure."[10] The optimism of modernity concerning human progress, what we can know with certainty and change with ingenuity, has been challenged and, some would say, debunked by the postmodern age. Apathy inevitably seeps into the soul when we, deep down, doubt if we can really know or change anything at all.

This pessimism concerning the human potential for knowing and doing, influenced by the cultural devaluation, deconstruction, and dismissal of foundational truth, has agitated the internal struggle many preachers endure regarding the validity of preaching. Now more than ever, preachers question if they have the authority or conviction to proclaim anything as ultimately true. "Does preaching still matter?" is a complex question lacking a unanimous answer. It's not easy to preach with passionate empathy for people when the preacher struggles to believe in the legitimacy, content, and transformative potential of preaching.

One of the ways the church counteracts the postmodern critique of preaching is to emphasize relevance. The life-application sermon is a popular device designed to connect biblical principles to topics the culture deems relevant. In the 1980s and 1990s, life-application sermons took flight and gained momentum. Sermons were considered relevant if they were immediately and practically applicable. The unchurched attended and the dechurched returned to hear "relevant" messages. Preaching found its voice again, so it seemed.

Then a problem surfaced. While these relevant sermons may have been full of good advice, they were generally void of God. In their worst moments, life-application sermons aimed at a utilitarian employment of God's biblical principles to make the listener's life happier not holier, more fulfilling but not necessarily more faithful. This kind of preaching interacted well with the "introspective, self-oriented approach to the art of living [that] was evident in the new wave of 'happiness' thinking that emerged in the late 1990s. Its key figures typically framed the search for happiness as an individualist pursuit that put personal satisfaction on a pedestal."[11]

The life-application preacher became an expert dispenser of practical principles dissected from the biblical metanarrative, a narrative prominently featuring a completely sovereign and loving God who creates, redeems, and restores. Listeners could subconsciously deduce from this sort of preaching that if one has God's principles for a better life, one doesn't really need God at all. These well-intentioned but *deistic sermons*[12] could be applied by the listener without any relational connection to or reliance upon God, and their finances, love life, and career would all still improve.

Deistic sermons are a recipe for apathetic disaster, in the preacher and the listener, because they disconnect preaching from the only source of power that makes it worthwhile: God. When the role of God in preaching is diminished, there is a loss of empathy in the preacher and the sermon because empathy is rooted in God. This loss fertilizes the ground where apathy grows. Apathetic preaching is void of authentic passion. It dispenses the type of good advice that any talk show host might offer. The problem is that preaching with apathy doesn't depend upon or proclaim God's empowering grace. The apathetic preacher comes across as nothing more than a noncommissioned salesperson with a laissez-faire "take it or leave it" posture.

A lack of preacher self-empathy is another contributor to apathetic preaching. If one cannot empathize with self, there will be a reduced capacity for empathy toward others.[13] Preachers are notoriously self-critical. A needless sense of shame and guilt often surfaces when life and ministry do not "come up roses." Many preachers endure a regular bout with the Monday morning blues, second-guessing their homiletic decisions from Sunday. Acute shame prevents the vulnerability necessary for empathy.[14] Regular self-loathing will make the most empathetic preachers apathetic in time; and any deformity in the preacher inevitably surfaces in the preaching.

Technology is suspect too. Those who are "plugged in" receive a constant bombardment of images and information depicting the problems of injustice and suffering via social media, TV, and electronic news sources. Technology allows us to voyeuristically glimpse local, national, and global pain. But does this peek into human pain cultivate empathy or apathy? Empathy expert Roman Krznaric asserts that the "barrage of depressing news stories and images from every corner of the planet" leads to the "empathy fatigue," which can foster apathy. Preachers can't help but be formed by this "empathy fatigue"[15] culture brought on, in part, by the information and imagery overload supplied by technology. Preachers are also deeply immersed in the distress of their congregants, which can cause an apathetic familiarity, numbness even, toward human suffering.

Technology is prone to perpetuating not only numbness but narcissism. The underbelly of social media is its tendency to inflict the curse of self-absorption upon users. Updating our e-status in order to present to the cyber world an image of our ideal self instead of our true self is destructive. The latent problem of social media is that it habituates users to think mostly of themselves most of the time. If one thinks constantly of oneself, there is little to no room for empathy toward others. According to Krznaric, "There is mounting evidence that the digital revolution, in its present form, is failing to send us on the path toward an empathic civilization."[16]

Apathy concerning human suffering, at least in part, is the result of online narcissism. Studies reveal that the more time people spend interacting on Facebook, the higher they score on narcissism tests.[17] The premier danger is that our *e-self* can dictate what the *actual* self becomes. Virtual reality becomes the tail that wags the dog of reality. Technology has created a world in which "our e-personality can drift toward narcissism, which then comes to infect our offline personality too."[18]

Honest Assessment

Although the church has had a track record of being countercultural in some of the ways that matter most, negative trends in culture do sometimes seep through the church's cracks. The skepticism, fatalism, and narcissism that permeate culture and produce apathy have, to some extent, leaked into the pew and the pulpit.

In the fall of 2000, one year before the 9/11 tragedy, James M. Lindsay wrote an article for *Foreign Affairs* titled "The New Apathy." He reflected, quite prophetically, on what it might take to overcome American apathy regarding our nation's foreign policy: "A renewed threat to American security would clearly do the trick."[19] One year later, 9/11 tragically did the trick. Now foreign policy, especially those dynamics that intersect national security, is chief among Americans' concerns.

The church is in the midst of a homiletic 9/11, a wake-up call that exposes the threat of apathy and the promise of empathy. A healthy wake-up call leads not to condemnation but liberation for the church.

Conclusion

Fruitful preachers recognize that being brutally honest about the bad news is a prerequisite that helps listeners fully embrace the good news when it arrives in the sermon. What I have outlined in this chapter regarding the hazards of cultural and homiletic apathy may seem gloomy, almost defeatist. The bad news of cultural callousness presented here is a precursor for the hopeful good news of homiletic empathy explored in the next chapter.

Chapter 2

A Case for Homiletic Empathy

Definitions and Descriptions

Finding a universally accepted definition of *empathy* can be as difficult as locating Bigfoot or spotting a unicorn. Still, let's consider a few possible definitions. Empathy is "an imaginative endeavor that results in us having the same type of feeling or emotion as the other person";[1] "the capacity to think and feel oneself into the inner life of another person";[2] or "an affective response more appropriate to another's situation than one's own."[3] However, Roman Krznaric's definition may be most helpful because it includes affective, cognitive, and behavioral dynamics. He writes, "empathy is the art of stepping imaginatively into the shoes of another person, understanding their feelings and perspectives, and using that understanding to guide your actions."[4] Empathy is the skill and, I contend, the grace that bridges the gap of distance between my reality and another's.

What does empathy have to do with preaching? Everything. Homiletic empathy is the grace that enables preachers to imagine their way into the situational shoes of others, to understand the thoughts and feel the emotions of listeners. Only then can they preach in a manner most responsive to their listeners' deepest needs. Homiletic empathy bridges the chasm between the preacher and the ethnically, generationally, educationally, economically, geographically, and spiritually diverse people to whom he or she preaches. Empathy turns a Bible study into a sermon. Empathy transforms

11

information into impact. Empathy enables intimacy between pulpit and pew. Yes, empathy matters!

APATHY		EMPATHY
Callous: does not feel concern for others	Affective	Passionate: feels concern for others
Disinterested: does not care to know the needs and perspectives of others	Cognitive	Curious: seeks to know the needs and perspectives of others
Passive: does not respond to the needs of others	Behavioral	Active: responds to the needs of others

Homiletic empathy is easier to describe than define. An old man in his seventies came to preach at a Christian college where I served as pastor. When I picked him up at the airport, I immediately felt sorry for the guy. I imagined students would nap through his sermon series. There was a huge gap of distance between this seventy-year-old brilliant Old Testament scholar and these eighteen- to twenty-two-year-olds, half of whom had no idea Zephaniah is a book in the Bible. Yet, despite the fact that he didn't sport a goatee, tattoos, or skinny jeans, he connected with students on a profound level. The impact of his words upon their lives surprised me and, I think, the students. I recall him voicing the doubts, hopes, and fears of college students with contextual precision, as if he himself were one of them. What did the late Dr. Dennis Kinlaw have that enabled his sermonic words to bridge the generational and educational gap between himself and his collegiate listeners? Empathy!

Safiyah was a well-educated African American woman in her thirties, appointed by her bishop to pastor a church in Iowa full of white rural folks, farmers mostly. Her education, ethnicity, and upbringing did not at all match the congregational demographics. This was the kind of "match" that makes us ponder what, or if, the bishop was thinking. Yet her preaching connected, and the church grew. How was the ethnic and geographic chasm overcome? Empathy!

Donovan is Caucasian, born and raised in the rural Midwest. He has been pastoring a church in urban Jersey City, New Jersey, for more than four decades. During most of his ministry there, he and his family have been the only white people in the church. His African American and Caribbean black congregants love him because he has found a way to articulate their dreams and disappointments for them through his preaching. What does Donovan have that allows him to leap the tall cultural fence between him and his congregants? Empathy!

I was a twenty-three-year-old college senior called to pastor a church in which the average age in the congregation was like 125. That's a stretch, but not much. I am an urbanite, born and bred in Philadelphia. That church was full of retirees from Podunk who had been following Christ three times longer than I had been alive. We could not be more dissimilar. Hard homiletic questions hounded me. How can I get past the naive nose on my face and jump into the scuffed-up pointy-toed shoes and bib overalls of senior men and the flowery dresses and knee-high stockings of elderly women? How can I articulate words that reflect not merely *my* preferences and perspectives but *their* particular thoughts and feelings? How in the name of Lawrence Welk and Johnny Carson can I put the gospel in a contextual container from which they can drink? Empathy!

In a cultural context of anger and apathy that results in callousness, a context in which the church has lost her power and privilege, how does the Christian preacher get a hearing? The present age demands not only exegesis or eloquence but empathy. The preacher who embodies with words and manner, in content and delivery, the empathy of God for the human race (chapter 3) will preach with amplified power. Empathy makes the homiletical world go 'round. But how much does empathy matter to preachers?

Though empathy is arguably the most important disposition necessary for fruitful preaching today, it seems to be flying under the radar of preachers who are on the prowl for skill development. There is, to my knowledge, no book written on the topic of preaching with empathy, which is why I wrote this one. I could only find a handful of book chapters or academic papers that name the topic at all. Empathy is a needle in the homiletic haystack for which only a few seem to be looking.

Not long ago, I conducted a brief survey on Facebook and Twitter. I asked the pastors among my friends and followers to respond to this question: What are the two or three most important skills necessary for preaching today? There were fifty-eight respondents. One of them replied, "Great hair and skinny jeans." Not the most helpful response. Only six of the fifty-eight respondents specifically cited empathy. That's only 10 percent. In all, 139 skills were mentioned. Only 12 of the 139 had any resemblance to empathy. That's only 8.6 percent. Clearly, empathy is not high on the list of preaching priorities. Without it, however, preaching falls flat.

Theological Anthropology

Your theological and anthropological leanings will dictate your level of hopeful optimism regarding the possibility of homiletic empathy. What you believe about God's grace and human nature will determine your receptivity to what follows.

Are humans naturally empathetic? Charles Darwin significantly influenced the thinking of those in the Western world over the past century and a half regarding this inquiry. Darwin argued that human beings are *homo self-centricus*, "primarily motivated by self-interest and an aggressive drive for self-preservation."[5] Natural selection was his argument in support of *homo self-centricus*. According to Darwin, the natural world, and all of her varied species, is built on a "survival of the fittest" mentality that fosters fierce competition, not empathic cooperation.

The Bible and Christian theology present a different picture of human essence than the one framed by some biologists. Humanity defiantly stumbled into a fallen state, starting in Genesis 3. In the depravity of sin and brokenness, humans tend to exhibit patterns of being and doing that support Darwinian *homo self-centricus*. Ever since Genesis 3, humanity has struggled with the kind of sinful self-absorption that led Cain to kill Abel and apathetically ask, "Am I my brother's keeper?" (Gen 4:9b, NIV). But the essential core of human nature, our true DNA, is rooted not in the fall of Genesis 3 but in the creation account of Genesis 1:27.

> God created humanity in God's own image,
>> In the divine image God created them,
>>> male and female God created them.

Note how the author of Genesis declared two times, in case the reader missed the first mention, that we humans are made in the *imago Dei*, the image of God.

Humans may bear the marks of the fall, but at a more essential level, we bear the image of God. God's "empathy-ometer," God's capacity to step into humanity's shoes, is off the charts. God's empathy is evidenced most powerfully by God's willingness, in Christ, to become one of us—and one *with* us despite the enormity of the sacrifice. To be made in God's image, then, means that we have the relationality of God *in* us. The Bible features an empathic God who, at every wayward turn in humanity's journey, ultimately chooses grace, mercy, and love as opposed to apathy. To be made in God's image, then, is to be naturally wired more for empathy than apathy. *Homo empathicus*, not *homo self-centricus*, is the core of who we are at creation.

To declare that humanity is made in the image of an empathic God (as we will discuss fully in chapter 3) is a statement about not just creation but redemption and restoration. We are not tethered to total depravity from now until the glorification that comes after the eschaton. If we believe we are born depraved beyond repair, that we are doomed to *homo self-centricus* in this life, we might as well throw up our hands apathetically about becoming empathetic. But if we believe Jesus came to swing the pendulum of humanity back before the fall of Genesis 3 to the creation of Genesis 1–2, it will change everything. If Christ came to restore the paradise lost in the fall *here* and *now*, not merely *there* and *later*, then we should be convinced that empathy overcomes apathy. In the words of Athanasius, "[Christ] became what we are so that we might become what he is."[6] Jesus came to redeem and restore what was lost in the fall. Any damage done by the fall is undone by the incarnation, life, death, resurrection, ascension, return, and reign of Christ. The person and work of Jesus Christ makes this return to "Eden" not just possible but probable. This high Christology is a trademark hope of the historic church.

Theologians often debate the ramifications of human depravity, but Christian theology overwhelmingly presents a more optimistic view of human nature than do modernists like Darwin, Hobbes, and Freud.[7] This triad emphasized a rather pessimistic and fatalistic view of the human condition. The church, on its best days, has been hopeful about the potency of God's grace to redeem and restore the paradise of Genesis 1–2 that was lost in the fall of Genesis 3. Despite the apathy so dominant in culture, the grace of God is at work like an invisible current below the surface leading the stream through the desert of depravity and back to the garden again.

You are what you believe. What a preacher intensely believes about divinity and humanity will often determine whether that preacher becomes apathetic or empathetic. If a preacher believes that God is an empathy-lacking, impassible judge and that humans are hopelessly depraved to the point of no return, apathy will take over like weeds in a garden. But when a Christo-centric theo-anthropology takes root, our homiletic convictions, dispositions, and practices will be infused with empathy for God and people.

Where one lands theologically is determined by what syllable of the biblical story gets the accent. The anthropological emphasis is placed either on the creation of the *imago Dei* in us described in Genesis 1 or on the fall and resultant depravity of Genesis 3. The former leads us back to the core of who we are, human beings made in the *imago Dei* with the empathic capacity of God deeply rooted in us.

Neuroscientific Support

Recent neuroscience confirms what the earliest words in the biblical story proclaim, that we humans are naturally more empathetic than apathetic—like the God in whose likeness we are made. Marco Iacoboni, a prominent neuroscientist at UCLA, concludes that humans are "wired for empathy"[8] based on his research of mirror neurons in the brain. Mirror neurons give humans the ability to, for example, read the pain on a person's face and actually feel that person's suffering. Iacoboni notes, "solid empirical evidence suggests that our brains are capable of mirroring the deepest aspects of the minds of others."[9] Mirror neurons give us the capacity to feel what someone else feels in the moment they feel it. A baby sees you smile and smiles back at you. You watch a 280-pound defensive end sack a quarterback from the blind side, and you wince in pain. That's baselevel empathy.

God has hardwired us for empathic relationality. A necessary requisite for any meaningful relationship is the mutual understanding that takes place between two people. The mirror neurons in the brain initiate and deepen concern for another person so that we are moved to act on their behalf. This finding leads Iacoboni to assert what Genesis 1 intimates— "morality is deeply rooted in our biology."[10] We are hardwired at creation with mirror neurons that enable empathy.

But didn't our human wiring get damaged by the fall and the corruption of the cosmos that followed it? Great question. There is another fascinating find in the field of neuroscience that relates to the brain's ability to be rewired for empathy. This finding corroborates another core Christian hope.

You might be thinking, *Empathy is hard for me. I'm too set in my ways to change at this stage of my life. The cement in my brain has dried.* The good news for you is that the brain's cement never completely dries. For decades, neurologists believed that the brain was fully formed in childhood and remained rather static thereafter. Recent studies prove otherwise. The brain is not static but plastic. "The brain does not settle into a rigid hard-wired state after childhood, but remains dynamic and malleable throughout life."[11] This is hopeful science for those who are not in the habit of being empathic.

The brain is malleable enough for us to be rewired back to our original design as *homo empathicus*.[12] This rewiring is actually visible. "The relationship between neuroplasticity and the development of empathy is now physiologically observable through brain imaging."[13] Neuroplasticity confirms that the human brain can be retrained, restored, and rebooted back to its original empathic design.

What neuroscience has recently discovered, Christian theology has proclaimed for two millennia. Although the wiring in our brain may have been damaged by the fall, our neurological predisposition toward empathic intimacy can be restored because God sent the Son, who sends the Spirit to the church. God restores the paradise lost so that we can be *homo empathicus* again. Through the Holy Spirit's sanctifying work in us, we are rebooted back to what we are at creation. Holy neurological pneumatology!

Mirror neurons confirm we are *wired* for empathy, created in God's image. Neuroplasticity confirms that we can be rewired for empathy, restored to God's image. This is the gospel of our Lord, Jesus Christ. And, we exclaim, thanks be to God!

Listening to Listeners

Oskar Schindler was a German businessman living during the Nazi regime. The movie *Schindler's List* portrays Schindler saving Jews despite the considerable personal risks and costs. When asked why he, a German, would care for Jews, he replied, "I knew the people who worked for me. When you know people, you have to behave toward them like human beings." Empathy, for Schindler and for the preacher, stems from knowing people. Knowing people intimately enough for the cultivation of empathy requires being present and attendant to people in our preaching context. Easier said than done.

Evidence suggests a disconnect between the pulpit and pew, the preacher and the people. The preacher still talks and the people still listen, but for empathy's sake the preacher must find a way to listen to the people talk. Dr. Lori Carrell surveyed preachers and their congregants to study the relationship between pulpit and pew. She published the results in her book *The Great American Sermon Survey*. The data revealed an acute disconnection. Out of the 102 pastors who completed the detailed survey, only one of them had a "formal procedure for involving listeners in sermon preparation."[14] Yet, when Carrell asked 479 listeners, "If you could get one message across to all preachers in the United States, what would it be?"

the second-highest response was essentially "know your listeners."[15] People want a preacher who relates to them. One of the primary problems with preaching today, according to Carrell's data, is a lack of empathy among preachers.

Listeners are most open to the sermon when they sense an empathic bond with the preacher. According to Carrell, few preachers build this kind of connection into the homiletic process. She wrote a follow-up book in response to the data from her survey titled *Preaching That Matters.* Carrell found that those who intentionally listened to congregants in order to know them more intimately and preach more incisively "made significant gains in the transformative quality of their sermons."[16] Empathic intimacy cultivated in the preacher toward congregants awakens the power latent in the preaching event. Yet, 87 percent of the preachers in Carrell's study prepare their sermons entirely in isolation.[17]

There are two preaching trends that contribute to the preacher's isolation from congregants. One is the dichotomization of the preacher's role between prophet for God and priest for people. Most preachers tend to perceive ourselves as prophets who represent a holy God to sinful people. The prophet preaches to confront, correct, and challenge people. The prophetic role is, of course, a necessary one; but perhaps we have leaned so far into that one role that the other side of the preaching coin has been shortchanged.

The preacher is not only called to be a bold prophet who represents God to people but an empathic priest who represents people to God. The priest preaches to intercede, advocate, atone, confess, and articulate for people. The prophetic *and* priestly roles are required in the preacher, or the congregation will become lopsided toward truth or grace, missing the beautiful blend of both.

Sermonic words must be faithful not only to the will and way of God (prophet) but to the hopes and hurts of humanity (priest). As we preach, people must feel as if we're articulating for them what they feel, know, and hope for but can't voice themselves. Listeners are most impacted not by eloquent or entertaining preachers but empathic ones. The empathic preacher puts to words for me what I feel deep in my soul but can't articulate. I would contend that the priestly empathy of Jesus drew people to him. The Samaritan woman at the well sensed that Jesus *knew* all about her, warts and all, and still loved her. She said to people in her town, "Come and see a man who has told me everything I've done!" (John 4:29a).

The second trend that leads to a relational disconnect between pulpit and pew is the specialization of the pastoral role. Today, even a midsize congregation might have on staff a teaching pastor, care pastor, outreach pastor, youth and children pastor, and maybe even an executive pastor to keep all the pastoral roles and responsibilities distinct. While there are benefits to pastoral specialization, there are major downsides too. One of the premier downsides of disintegrating the pastoral roles of caring, leading, preaching, and so on is the dilution of empathy. It is quite fashionable today for the preaching pastor to spend twenty to thirty hours in isolation from people in order to craft sermons and work with the "worship production team." The assumption is that those who listen to our sermons can get in the way of sermon preparation if we let them. Specialty preachers may be rhetorically eloquent, but if they lack the eloquence of empathy, the sermon's impact will be diminished.

I would contend that the most fruitful preachers in the church are not the visionary kings or clerical CEOs, who sit in spacious offices cloistered off from regular folk. No, the best preachers are empathic shepherds who incarnationally go out to the fields where the sheep dwell; their words are sheep-scented.

The church I most recently served as lead pastor had a growth spurt; it tripled in size in seven years. There were many reasons why the church grew into an ethnically, economically, generationally, and educationally diverse body. Some, though I humbly admit not all, would say that preaching was one of the ministries that influenced the increase. The people who seemed to appreciate my preaching the most did not cite my rhetorical skill (another confession) but my empathic connection to the diversity of people God brought to us. They wouldn't use the term *empathic* to describe my preaching, but that's what they meant. "I feel like he gets me....He comes across as one among and not above the congregation....He puts into words what I experience but can't express."

The problem, however, was that I allowed the trend toward specialization to infiltrate my ministry and reduce my empathy. This weakened my preaching. The more the church grew, the more time I spent cloistered in my study isolated from people. When I stood up to preach I felt awkwardly severed from my people, like a substitute teacher. My sermons had, I think, eloquence and exegesis but not much empathy. I lacked the passion and power that results from being empathically in touch with the congregation. When I leaned into the trend toward specialization, which for me meant isolation, I experienced some of my worst days in ministry. Thankfully, I learned the importance of empathy, albeit the hard way.

Conclusion

The best preachers are not the best talkers but the best listeners. They sit and listen to the heart of humanity. Then, on Sundays, they stand and deliver words that show the scars of soul-level listening. The deep-in-the-pulpit cries out to the deep-in-the-pews. "Deep called to deep" (Ps 42:7a).

I visited the Kwanglim United Methodist Church in Seoul, South Korea, during my doctoral studies. The size of the congregation at the time was fifty thousand members. Despite the congregation's enormity, every member received an annual pastoral visit. I accompanied a pastor on one of these home visits. A translator accompanied me.

The young pastor sat on the floor across from his elderly female host. After a bit of small talk (with fifty thousand members there's not much of it), the pastor asked, "What are your prayer requests?" The woman shared about the good, bad, and ugly of her life, as the pastor listened intently. After five minutes, she stopped. The pastor sat reflectively for another two minutes, listening to God after he listened to the woman. Then he preached a seven-minute homily applied specifically to the situations of her life. Because he listened empathically, he spoke profoundly.

Empathy empowers the preacher to congruently embody the gospel of Jesus Christ. God empathically stepped into time and space, into flesh, blood, and bone, to prove God's solidarity with us. We further explore the beauty of this empathic God in the next chapter.

Part II: Pouring the Foundation

Chapter 3

Empathic God

Is Divine Empathy Possible?

W hat preachers believe about God will ooze out through the pores of their preaching. If we view God as a cosmic sheriff waiting for people to mess up so God can punish them, it will come through in our preaching. If we are convinced that God is a sentimental softy with no standards for holiness, it will surface in our preaching. If we preachers believe in a God of truth and grace, justice and mercy, it will seep through our preaching pores. Developing and delivering sermons is not just a practical task; it is chiefly a theological one. Our preaching discloses our theology and shapes the theology of the people to whom we preach. This homiletic challenge thrills and scares the conscientious preacher.

Critical to the topic of empathy is the long-running theological debate concerning whether God is capable of feeling and suffering. *Impassibilists* believe God is incapable of emotion. God is unchangeable and, therefore, can't be moved by external forces. God is independent of anything outside Godself so "must be incapable of suffering, for suffering is always caused by something else."[1] *Passibilists*, on the other hand, believe that God is *emotive*, that God somehow feels love and pain. God isn't forced or manipulated into responsiveness. God freely chooses to absorb suffering without being overcome by it. If God is love, then God must be capable of suffering. Love inevitably suffers.[2]

Divine impassibility is the traditional view, asserted early in the Christian movement by the church fathers, specifically the Cappadocians. They were highly influenced by the Greek philosophy of the Hellenistic world in which they lived. The Stoic philosophy of their day denigrated emotion as "a disease of the soul" and celebrated apathy because it "guaranteed an undisturbed operation of the rational mind."[3] Stoic apathy enables one to be unmoved, unaffected, and uninterrupted by emotions that result from pleasure or pain. Greek mythology portrayed the gods as emotionally vulnerable to human manipulation. Apathy, then, was considered an ideal of perfection that protected one from manipulation. The church fathers applied this idealized apathy to their doctrine of God (divine *apatheia*). Their goal was to defend God's transcendence, but they may have inadvertently minimized God's immanence.

Divine passibility is the belief in a God who does feel pleasure and pain, not as a passive victim but as a willing participant. God isn't forced to suffer but chooses to do so. Passibilism is rooted not in speculative philosophy, as is impassibility, but in the biblical narrative.[4] The Bible depicts God as one who is compassionate (Ex 34:6), jealous (Ex 20:5), and even wrathful (Hos 11:9), to name just a few of the many emotive characteristics attributable to God. Of course, the most often cited passion of God from Genesis to Revelation is love. And love, as any friend, parent, or spouse knows, makes one emotionally vulnerable to the suffering of the beloved.

Impassibility is a theological position based primarily on tradition and reason, while passibility is rooted predominantly in scripture and experience. An impassible God is apathetic to the pleasure and pain that exists outside of Godself. A passible God is empathetic to the pleasure and pain that exists outside of Godself. The preacher who is convinced of the impassibility of God, his *apatheia*, will stress divine sovereignty, transcendence, power, and justice. The preacher who views God as passible will emphasize divine love, mercy, and, yes, empathy. Perhaps the goal is to emphasize both sides without neglecting either in our preaching.

The theological direction toward which one leans will impact one's level of empathy. Research data confirms the intimate connection between theology, what one believes, and empathy, how one behaves. Almost six thousand religiously diverse adolescents (ages thirteen through fifteen) in the United Kingdom were subjects in the study. Researchers were testing the linkage between images of God and empathy levels. The findings showed that students who imagined God as merciful, moved by external need, had higher empathy scores than those who envisioned God primarily as just.[5] Theology regulates empathy.

To be fair, theologians in the divine impassibility camp affirm the relationality of God. If, however, God is impassibly apathetic, unmoved by beings outside Godself, how can God be relational? Edward Farley's question is justified. "How can we account for God's active relation to the world in the light of attributes that seem to remove God from time, change, and responsiveness?"[6] God is relational. The most prevalent metaphors for God in scripture are relational ones (i.e., father, mother, husband, friend). In order for God to be authentically relational, God must be passible. And, if God is relational God must be empathetic, since empathy is "the glue that makes social life possible"[7] and holds relationships together. Those who score lowest on empathy tests, such as sociopaths or narcissists, have the hardest time sustaining healthy and meaningful relationships.

God is love, so God suffers.[8] Jurgen Moltmann says, "A God who cannot suffer is poorer than any man. For a God who is incapable of suffering is a being who cannot be involved."[9] God is relational and, thus, risks being moved by external forces. God chooses to absorb cosmic pain, but is not diminished by it. This view of God is more Hebraic (biblical) than Hellenic (philosophical).

The rest of this chapter builds on the case for divine empathy by exploring the Trinity, incarnation, and ministry of Jesus. The chapter concludes with practical preaching implications based on God's empathy.

The Trinity

Perhaps a middle way that brings together *impassibilists* and *passibilists* is the recognition that God is empathic from eternity and before creation. Empathy is not caused in God but is God's nature. Creation is the consequence, not the cause, of divine empathy. But this begs the question, how could God express empathy when God alone existed?

Within the Trinity, there is empathy. Empathy, then, is God's eternal nature. While this assertion may seem unsettled, the use of the term *perichoresis* to describe how the persons of the godhead relate to each other is not. The term is closely related to *perichoreuo*, which literally means "to dance in a circle." Catherine Mowry LaCugna describes the trinitarian dance as "one fluid motion of encircling, encompassing, permeating, enveloping, outstretching... an eternal movement of giving and receiving.... The divine dance is fully personal and interpersonal, expressing the essence and unity of God."[10] Gregory of Nazianzus introduced *perichoresis* into his theology of the Trinity back in the fourth century CE, and the word has maintained its essential meaning. The church through the ages has overwhelmingly embraced it.

There are various descriptions to explain *perichoresis,* but practically all of them accent the interpenetration, interconnectedness, and interdependence of the Father, Son, and Spirit. What is implicit in this language, John Jefferson Davis makes explicit. He argues that *perichoresis* involves "reciprocal empathy," noting that empathy is "the ability to feel another's experience."[11] The persons of the Trinity open themselves to each other, enabling them to think and feel what the others think and feel. The pleasure and pain of one of them is, in some way, experienced by all of them. So, as Moltmann argues, as "the Son suffers dying, the Father suffers the death of the Son."[12] *Perichoretic communion* is a "heart-in-heart connection between two or more persons characterized by reciprocal empathy."[13]

Before the trinitarian God empathically "so loved the world," God was empathic love. Wolfhart Pannenberg wrote, "From all eternity the Father loves the Son, the Son loves the Father, and the Spirit loves the Father in the Son and the Son in the Father."[14] Empathic connection plays out in the life of Jesus Christ, captured best in the Johannine literature. Jesus stated bluntly, "I am in the Father and the Father is in me" (John 14:11). Later in John's Gospel, Jesus prayed that his disciples would experience with God and each other the oneness he enjoys with the Father (John 17:20-23). The role of the Spirit in all of this is crucial. According to Jesus, the Holy Spirit is the empathic adhesive that connects disciples into *perichoretic communion* with God and each other (John 14:15-31; 1 John 3:24).

Divine empathy has no boundaries. Although it starts in the center of God, it moves with centrifugal force to the margins, "toward any and all in need."[15] When God created humanity "in God's own image" (Gen 1:26-27), there was an immediate empathic vibe from God toward people, much like what a mother feels for her newborn baby. Empathy is not ultimately interior. It's the impetus for God creating, sustaining, and redeeming the world. The empathy that exists within the Trinity extends to (salvation), in (sanctification), and through (mission) the church.

The Incarnation

The most empathic move in the history of the world is summed up in the Apostle John's claim "the Word became flesh and made his home among us" (John 1:14a). That's one empathic leap! The definitive extension of Trinitarian empathy is the incarnation of the Son. God's heart broke at the pain and angst of the human condition, the complete corruption of the cosmos. God's empathy crossed unfathomable boundaries. God, through the Son, took on flesh, blood, and bone to become one of us and one with us. By God's voluntary suffering love, God did for us what we could not do for ourselves. Pure empathy!

A scene in the 2001 movie *Wit* powerfully depicts incarnational empathy. The story centers on Dr. Vivian Bearing, a brilliant but abrasive university professor of English literature, who undergoes chemotherapy treatments and other painful procedures. Most medical professionals have no empathy for her. Their apathy toward her pain leads her to flashbacks of times when she lacked empathy toward the people in her life, particularly students. Now that she is suffering, she longs for an intimate empathic connection with people. Intimacy evades her for the better part of the film.

Finally, at the end of the movie, Vivian receives the gift of empathy. Stuck in a hospital bed, alone and frightened by her mortality, she receives a visit from her former English professor and mentor, Dr. Ashford. The professor walks in and sees the anguish and fear all over Vivian's face. Empathy surfaces immediately in Ashford.

What this woman, who looks to be at least seventy years old, does next is profound. She slips off her shoes and struggles her way onto Vivian's hospital bed. Lying with Vivian in this bed of pain, Ashford reads a book she brought as a gift, *The Runaway Bunny*. This children's story is about a bunny who wanted to run away from home and a mother who promises to find her runaway bunny wherever he goes. The little bunny pledges to become a trout and hide from his mother. She promises to become a fisherman and catch him. Then the persistent bunny threatens to hide by becoming a rock on a mountain. Mother bunny assures him she will become a rock climber and "climb to where you are." The runaway bunny says he will become a crocus in a hidden garden. The momma bunny pledges to become a gardener in order to find her little bunny. This back and forth goes on for a few more pages until the runaway bunny realizes there is nowhere he can run or hide where his mom won't find him. She will incarnationally go where she needs to go and become what she needs to be in order to find him.[16]

This story about a maternal bunny's willingness to become whatever the situation demands in order to locate her baby, coupled with Dr. Ashford's physical move onto the bed of Vivian's suffering is a vivid illustration of God's empathic incarnation among us. Ever since Genesis 3, God went on a mission to reconnect with the human race. God sent the law; that didn't work out so well. God sent the prophets; that went south. Finally, in the fullness of time, God, reminiscent of the runaway bunny's mother, became what we needed God most to become in order to redeem and restore us. And it was divine empathy that drove God to these great lengths. The incarnation is God's empathic solidarity with humanity. Social scientists would call this "a radical social experiment." Christians call it "the gospel."

The Ministry of Jesus

The Gospels depict a Jesus who was driven by empathy, not only for the Father as discussed above, but for humanity. The Greek word close in meaning to empathy is *splagchnizomai*, usually translated "compassion." The term literally means the inner parts of the body, such as the lungs, heart, liver, and kidneys. In time, the word denoted the seat of the affections. *Splagchnizomai*, then, is a deep-in-the-bowels-of-the-body ache that one feels because of another's situation.

The word is used a dozen times in the Gospels, nine times to indicate that Jesus was "moved" or "filled" with compassion. When compassion welled up in Jesus, he healed the sick (Matt 14:14), fed the hungry (Matt 15:32ff.; Mark 8:2ff.), gave sight to the blind (Matt 20:34), touched a leper (Mark 1:41), taught the crowd (Mark 6:34), and comforted a grieving mother (Luke 7:13). In Jesus, empathy was a God-given capacity to physically, emotionally, and spiritually feel his way into another's situation so that he acted on that person's behalf. Jesus's empathy was not merely a warm fuzzy but an internal disposition that led to external action. In Jesus's case, empathic behavior led him to the cross. Christian empathy is an internal disposition that leads to an external response for the sake of someone else and often entails suffering.

Two of the best-known heroes from the stories Jesus told in Luke's Gospel were marked by extreme, even shocking empathy. The good Samaritan is one of these heroes (10:25-37). At the time Jesus told the parable, Samaritans and Jews despised each other. The races had much in common, but their few differences divided them. Yet, the Samaritan man, not the Jewish men (priest and Levite), was the one who felt empathy for the presumably Jewish victim who was half dead on the road. Jesus told this parable about a heroic Samaritan to a Jewish audience. Empathy toward enemies, or even people different from us "on the other side of the road," is challenging and commendable. The Samaritan man admirably overcame the prevalent racism of the day to empathize with a person not like him. The good Samaritan sacrificed time, money, and energy to help the helpless victim (10:33-35). Like God through the incarnation, the Samaritan empathically crossed boundaries in response to human need.

Five chapters later in Luke, Jesus told another story about radical empathy. The parable of the prodigal son is as much about an empathetic father and his apathetic older son as it is about the reckless younger son. From a distance, the father saw his younger son return from rebellion. The father didn't feel anger or apathy, according to the text, but empathy. The father experienced *splagchnizomai*: he "was moved with compassion" for his son (Luke 15:20). And, as it was with Jesus and the good Samaritan, empathy led to action. It always does. The father ran to his son, embraced, and kissed him. Then, he threw a party for this wayward son who staggered home. Empathy is clearly "more than a feeling," to quote the Boston song; it is ultimately expressed as an external response on behalf of a person or group in need.[17]

The Gospels depict the ministry of Jesus, but the book of Hebrews describes it. The pages of Hebrews are drenched with the empathy of Jesus,[18] but one particular passage stands out. Hebrews 4 focuses prominently on the empathy-saturated ministry of Jesus (vv. 14-16). The author writes about Jesus, "For we do not have a high priest who is unable to empathize with our weakness, but we have one who has been tempted in every way, just as we are—yet he did not sin" (v. 15, NIV). Theologians tend to focus on this verse's assertion of Jesus's purity, what distinguishes him from humanity, and not on his empathy, what connects him to humanity. Yet, even a casual reading of Hebrews reveals that the primary focal point of the book is the empathy of Jesus and his ministry. God felt empathy for "the Hebrews," a group constantly harassed and oppressed by the more powerful nations among them. God acted on their behalf through Jesus Christ. Jesus is both the high priest *and* the sacrifice of a new covenant between divinity and humanity.

Jesus embodied and emphasized empathy. He lived it and longed for it in others. Empathy is not about being nice or harmonious. Jesus's empathy drove him to seek freedom and justice for all, even if it meant going into the temple and boldly confronting injustice (Mark 11:12-26). His empathy liberated and dignified people, particularly those on the societal margins. He empathically bridged the huge chasm of distance between divinity and humanity. Preachers are summoned by this empathic God to do the same through the practice of Christian preaching.[19]

More Practical Preaching Implications

Divine passibility, trinitarian perichoresis, and *incarnational contextualization* are theological concepts that shape the practice of preaching. Theology and practice are two sides of the same coin for the thoughtful preacher. Chapters 5 and 6 will focus entirely on practical ways to preach with empathy, but let's consider here some practical implications from our theological exploration.

Implications of Divine Passibility

God is passible in that God allows Godself to be moved by external forces, mostly the needs of the human race. The unchanging God faithfully responds with empathic power to human hopes and hurts. This is not a compromise but a consequence of God's nature.

Preachers need to take our cues from God. We do this when we allow the needs of the people to whom we preach shape the why, what, and how we preach, even if outside the box of our stylistic preferences. Sometimes we make our preferred preaching style more important than listener needs. The impassible preacher might preach truth, but likely without the grace of empathic concern. If God accommodates and adjusts to human need, so will the theologically faithful preacher.

James taught the fifth-grade Sunday school class in one of the churches I pastored. He was committed to the task. He was always on time and ready to teach. As anyone who has worked with kids knows, that's a big deal. The only problem was that every class turned into a hellfire and brimstone lesson designed to scare kids into conversion. Some kids were converted weekly! The class dwindled from a couple dozen kids to just a handful. I had a tactful talk with James, imploring him to adjust to the needs of his small flock before it became even smaller. I suggested that while older kids might be able to handle his style, fifth graders struggled. He shot back, "Well, Pastor, that's my style and I can't change at this point. Maybe you should find someone else to teach." I did. He meant well, but his teaching style trumped listener needs, revealing a lack of empathy.

Pastoral confession alert! I've done what James did, but for different reasons. In my second year of pastoral ministry, I served two congregations. I was the solo pastor of a small rural congregation, consisting mostly of members in their seventies. At the same time, I was the youth pastor at a large church in a college town. I was burning the candle on both ends, and empathy was the casualty. There were times, I confess, when I preached the same exact sermon in the same exact way for both groups. Of course, what I said may have been true, but it was not really *for* one of the groups. My sermon preparation, content, and delivery was impassible, unmoved by particular congregational dynamics like age, ethnicity, education, economics, and spirituality. Empathy makes listener needs central and preacher preferences peripheral.

Implications of Trinitarian Perichoresis

We explored how the Father, Son, and Spirit interact with each other in a *perichoretic* dance of sorts. They are mutually interconnected in ways that foster empathic connection between them. God invites us to experience this kind of communion with the Trinity and, in turn, with each other in Christian community. "Being made in the image of God is to be constituted with the capacity for *perichoresis*."[20] Preaching, including preparation, content, and delivery, that is faithful will evidence the preacher's *perichoresis* with God and the ecclesial community.

How can the preacher embody *perichoresis* with God and others in the practice of preaching? For starters, if preachers are *in* the Father and the Son while being possessed by the Spirit, the ministry of preaching is not engaged alone *for* God but in communion *with* God. Pastoral burnout is widespread. Preaching fatigue is a real problem. Preachers who perceive and practice their ministry as an outflow of *perichoretic* communion with the Trinity are more likely to flourish for the long-haul than the preacher who flies solo.[21]

The means of grace are avenues through which God invites us into *perichoretic* communion. John Wesley separated the means of grace into two categories, works of piety and works of mercy. The works of piety have a vertical orientation, facilitating one's empathic connection to God. They include praying, participating in the Eucharist, reading scripture, and fasting. The works of mercy happen horizontally, increasing one's empathic relation to people. Feeding the hungry, practicing hospitality, clothing the naked, and visiting the imprisoned constitute some of the acts of mercy. As the works of piety connect us to the empathy of God, the works of mercy empathically move us to people in need.[22] This is how the stream of *perichoretic* empathy flows.

Perichoretic communion with the congregation has practical application too. Preachers benefit by finding ways to preach that are mutually interdependent and interconnected with the staff and laity. About ten years into my ministry, it occurred to me that this was important. So, during our midweek staff meeting, I began the practice of reading the preaching text and inviting a diversity of voices to offer observations and raise questions about the text or topic I would tackle on Sunday. They frequently saw what I missed and always influenced what I preached.

Trinitarian perichoresis is a theological concept loaded with practical implications, but space limits us to the exploration of just one more that is crucial for preachers. If the Christian community, like the members of the Trinity, are really "in" each other, we will empathically "rejoice with those who rejoice, weep with those who weep" (Rom 12:15, NRSV). As preachers get caught up in the *perichoretic* trinitarian dance, we will cooperate and not compete with each other in ministry. *Perichoresis* invites us into the ministry of others. When my sisters and brothers succeed in preaching, so do I. When they struggle, I do too.

There are numerous practical ways to embody mutuality in ministry. Alcoholics Anonymous has given us one. The common purpose around which all members unite is to get and stay sober. They pursue this goal mutually. Every member needs a sponsor and, hopefully in time, will become a sponsor. The sponsors and "sponsees" become partners in the quest toward sobriety.

What if preachers were as mutually interdependent and interconnected as the AA sponsor and sponsee? Try to identify a sponsor, a mentor, who can walk with you through the ups and downs of the preaching life. Additionally, invest in a preaching sponsee, a mentee, who can benefit from your listening ear and ministry experience.[23] There are numerous hazards, as well as joys, that come with the preaching life. The hazards are cut in half and the joys doubled when we share them with others.

Implications of Incarnational Contextualization

God's manner of empathic connection is incarnation. He jumped into human skin. He came onto our turf. He came to first-century Jews as a first-century Jew. He "made his home" among them. Sitting where they sat, walking where they walked, working where they worked, and worshipping where they worshipped, enabled the enfleshed God to preach from and into peoples' lives. "He knew all people" and "knew what human nature was" (John 2:24-25). Jesus got up close and personal with people enough to know them. Therefore, he could minister precisely based on the particularities of the people he served. Jesus was able to imagine his way into the situational sandals of others because he spent time with them on their turf.

In chapter 2, I asserted that preachers make a major mistake when we isolate ourselves from congregants. Is it even possible for a preacher who spends every single moment of sermon preparation cloistered behind a closed door to empathically connect with people during the preaching event? I doubt it. Following the example of Christ, the preacher comes to know people by dwelling among them. When we know our people well, we can serve our people best.

Incarnational contextualization draws my mind to the practice of method acting. Method actors work hard to match the psychological and, at times, the physical states of the characters they play. The goal is to empathize deeply with the character so they can authentically represent that character.

Daniel Day-Lewis is one of the most gifted method actors. He will make significant sacrifices to put himself into the situational shoes of the characters he portrays. In 1989, Day-Lewis played Christy Brown in the film *My Left Foot*. Brown had cerebral palsy and could only use his left foot. During the filming, Day-Lewis stayed in character. On the set, he stayed in a wheelchair and the crew had to push him around. They also had to spoon-feed Day-Lewis his meals. *The Daily Telegraph* describes his legendary quest for empathy in other roles:

> Playing Gerry Conlon in *In the Name of the Father*, Day-Lewis lived on prison rations to lose 30 pounds, spent extended periods in the jail cell on set, went without sleep for two days, was interrogated for three days by real policemen, and asked that the crew hurl abuse and cold water at him. For *The Boxer* in 1997, he trained for weeks with the former world champion Barry McGuigan, who said that [Day-Lewis] became good enough to turn professional. The actor's injuries include a broken nose and a damaged disc in his lower back.[24]

The Son of God immersed himself in the pain and angst, joys and delights of the human condition so that he might faithfully represent us to the Father, not to mention the Father to us.

Incarnational contextualization requires empathy. Like the method actor who spends time in the context of the character he plays, the preacher must go onto the turf of those who constitute the preaching event. Only when the preacher expends the time and energy to dwell among the people can he or she empathically reflect, through sermonic words, what it's like to be them. We "learn" the listeners best by going where they work, live, shop, play, heal, and suffer. We ask them questions to help us imagine their reality; then we listen. Empathic listening to the lives of congregants will help the preacher to preach with incarnational insight. Dietrich Bonhoeffer sums it up well: "We should listen with the ears of God that we may speak the Word of God."[25]

Chapter 4

Exemplars of Empathic Preaching

History Matters

In his introduction to Athanasius's fourth-century work *On the Incarnation*, C. S. Lewis shares the following insight:

> Every age has its own outlook. It is specially good at seeing certain truths and specially liable to make certain mistakes. We all, therefore, need the books that will correct the characteristic mistakes of our own period. And that means the old books. All contemporary writers share to some extent the contemporary outlook—even those, like myself, who seem most opposed to it.[1]

Lewis is asserting the importance of learning from the past to move forward in the present. Inviting historical figures and ideas into current conversations can prevent contemporary tunnel vision. The empathic preachers of yesterday confirm and confront the preaching practices of today. While many of the opportunities for preaching with empathy are specific to their time, the homiletical wisdom of yesterday has much to offer.

The preachers of the past have much to teach us. From some, we learn how to preach with biblical and theological depth. Others exemplify how to structure sermons with purposeful design. Then, there are those who show us how to preach with empathy. The empathic exemplars we consider in this chapter aren't perfect. Everyone has chinks in their homiletic armor. Our two exemplars, though, found a way to get past the self-absorbed nose on their faces to the needs of the people among them. Their empathic preaching empowered people to transform social structures and remedy societal ills. Their preaching changed the trajectory of the world for the better. Empathic Christian preaching has that kind of potential!

John Wesley (1703–91)

Context

"Rarely has a Christian preacher spoken to the need of his day quite so profoundly as John Wesley."[2] Wesley is known as the founder of Methodism, a movement that generally attracted poor, uneducated, and unchurched people. A vast gap of difference existed between Wesley and the people who were converted, nurtured, and empowered through his preaching.

John Wesley was highly educated. He studied theology at Christ Church College of Oxford University, one of the most prestigious academic institutions of the day. He was ordained as an Anglican priest. His love of learning was evidenced by his unanimous election to a teaching position at Oxford's Lincoln College in 1926.

While Wesley was neck-deep in the elitist circles of the Church of England and Oxford University, England's poor were getting poorer. The Industrial Revolution initiated significant population growth in urban areas, as workers fled the farm for the factory. In time, many became unemployed as machines replaced people.

The Church of England, catering to the societal upper crust, was apathetic about ameliorating the problems of poverty and alcoholism. The elite congregated comfortably in ecclesiastical huddles. The church, by and large, lacked missional empathy.

These dynamics set the stage for an unlikely connection between an Oxford-educated Anglican priest like John Wesley and the uneducated poor who became the first Methodists. "The rift...between the rich and the poor, the educated and the ignorant, the religious and the irreligious had by the middle of the eighteenth century become a chasm." Yet, Wesley's preaching connected across the divide with "coal miners, mill workers, and scrub maids...to prisoners, to soldiers, and to mobs."[3] Empathy established the connection.

Empathy

John Wesley preached his first open-air sermon in Bristol on April 2, 1739. Up until that point, he felt field-preaching was "strange," because it happened outside of ecclesiastical walls.[4] Wesley, until his dying day, considered himself a proper Anglican. So, what would possess him to engage in what he called the "vile" practice of field-preaching for fifty-one years,[5] despite the hazards he endured because of it?[6] Was it the arm-twisting of his friend George Whitefield? Perhaps the impetus for his field-preaching was the closed church doors that were slammed in his face because of his "unfashionable"[7] doctrine of sanctification. Or maybe Wesley was compelled to engage in this unusual sort of preaching because of the extraordinary results it produced.

In his *A Farther Appeal to Men of Reason and Religion*, Wesley makes the case for field-preaching from a theology of divine empathy. "Yet the Shepherd of souls sought after us into the wilderness…ought not we also to seek…and to save that which was lost? Behold the amazing love of God to the outcasts of men! His tender condescension to their folly!"[8] According to Wesley, the essential nature of God is empathic love for those wandering around hopelessly in the wilderness of life. And, if necessary, God will go "out of the usual way to save the souls which he has made,"[9] even if it happens in the field not the sanctuary.

Theology cultivated empathy in Wesley. His conception of God as love cultivated God's love in Wesley. Empathy for the poor and unchurched of his day led Wesley to an incarnational "on their turf" approach to preaching. The divine empathy that brought Christ incarnationally to the world was at work in and through Wesley since "renewal in the image of God entails being drawn into God's likeness."[10] Wesley articulated his empathic concern for the marginalized masses:

> …who, week after week, spent the Lord's day, either in the ale-house, or in idle diversions, and never troubled themselves about going to church, or to any public worship at all. Now, would you really have desired that these poor wretches should have sinned on until they dropped into hell? Surely you would not. But by what other means was it possible they should have been plucked out of the fire?…It is hard to conceive anything else which could have reached them. Had it not been for field-preaching…they must have run on in the error of their way, and perished in their blood.[11]

Divine empathy got the best of Wesley, via the process of sanctification, and led him to engage in the "vile" practice of field-preaching.

Empathy enhanced Wesley's preaching. George Whitefield was widely considered the more rhetorically eloquent and entertaining preacher. He had more charisma and, usually, larger crowds than Wesley. So what allowed Wesley's preaching to have such lasting impact? O. C. Edwards Jr. offers, "Perhaps it was something about his presence, the sort of overwhelming compassionate concern" that came through Wesley when he preached.[12] Empathy has the power, it seems, to make an average preacher good and a good preacher great.

Wesley's Practices

Empathy derives from theology and drives practices. Wesley's preaching practices were transformed by his empathy for people on the fringes. Every preacher has preferences. So did Wesley, who admitted, "What marvel the devil does not love field-preaching! Neither do I: I love a commodious room, a soft cushion, an handsome pulpit."[13] Empathy for people overcame his preaching preferences in important, practical ways.

Wesley was a brilliant scholar. He taught Greek and was skilled in biblical exegesis. But academic excellence and rhetorical eloquence were given a backseat so that his preaching was adaptable, accessible, anecdotal, and applicable to the uneducated poor.

Adaptable. Wesley's preaching was adaptable. He would not impose his preaching style across contexts. He preached differently, for example, to the elite in St. Mary's Church at Oxford than he did to coal miners in the fields of Bristol. John Hampson, Wesley's first biographer, notes, "Wesley's manner was graceful and easy . . . his style neat, simple, perspicuous, and admirably adapted to the capacity of his hearers."[14] What Wesley may have lacked in communication charisma, he made up for in empathic adaptability. Fruitful preachers seem willing to adapt their style to listener needs. Those who don't adapt become a rotary phone in a smartphone world. The goal is not compromise or condescension but the bull's-eye of contextualization.

Accessible. Adaptable preachers proclaim the gospel in a manner that is accessible. In the preface to his published sermons, Wesley articulates what was his most well-known preaching practice: "I design plain truth for plain people."[15] He admits, "For I now write, as I generally speak, *ad populum*—to the bulk of mankind, to those who neither relish nor understand the art of speaking."[16] Preachers must resist the temptation to showcase our learning, especially fresh out of seminary, so that we can put the gospel in an accessible container from which our people can drink. What appeared to consume Wesley more than his preferred preaching style was what listeners needed to grow in grace.

Anecdotal. Surprisingly, Wesley's preaching was anecdotal. One is hard-pressed to locate anecdotal illustrations in Wesley's published sermons, but his oral sermons were apparently full of them. His published sermons were designed to nurture faith, while his oral sermons were aimed at initiating faith. He preached evangelistic sermons in the fields but wrote discipleship sermons for publication. So, the latter are clearly void of the emotionally charged anecdotes for which Wesley was known. A sophisticate of the day came, out of curiosity, to hear Wesley preach. He was critical of Wesley's "vulgar enthusiasm" and telling of "stories."[17] Another educated listener noted that Wesley "told many excellent stories."[18] I would argue, based on his theology, spirituality, and ministry to the poor, that empathy made Wesley a bit emotional and highly passionate about connecting divine empathy with human need. He was, after all, pejoratively labelled an "enthusiast."

Applicable. Wesley's sermons were applicable. "The tendency to select topics according to the context and audience, and speak to their needs and at their level" was supported by those who observed Wesley's preaching.[19] Wesley, and the Methodist movement, sought to change not just the heads and hearts of people, but their habits as well. Sermons can cross the line into the realm of overly prescriptive and mandated application. Wesley's sometimes did. But in his particular context, when many longtime churchgoers were more prone to discuss Christianity than practice it, prescriptive application made sense. In a twenty-first-century North American context, descriptive application is more palatable than that which is prescriptively mandated.

What Wesley embodied in his preaching, he encouraged for Methodist preachers. He advised preachers to "always suit your subject to your audience"[20] and to look upon listeners with "an air of affection and regard."[21] Some preachers of Wesley's day, and ours too, preached *at* listeners with anger or *past* listeners with apathy. To the contrary, "Wesley spoke very directly *to* listeners,"[22] [emphasis mine] as a sign of empathic respect. Preachers in the Methodist movement were equipped to preach sermons that were adaptable, accessible, anecdotal, and applicable to people ostracized by the Church of England. Overall, "Wesley taught speakers to love their listeners...a radical notion,"[23] certainly for his day and perhaps even for our own.

Martin Luther King Jr. (1929–68)

Context

Martin Luther King Jr.'s father, grandfather, and great-grandfather were Baptist preachers.[24] His father became pastor of the Ebenezer Baptist Church in Atlanta, Georgia, shortly after Martin was born. In that church context, the young King saw the power of Christian preaching to dignify the downcast. The church deepened King's faith.

Educational opportunities broadened King's mind. He studied at Morehouse College in Atlanta and Crozer Seminary near Philadelphia, before receiving his PhD in systematic theology from Boston University. His world was enlarged as he encountered people and places beyond his black, Southern church roots.

Despite the passing of desegregation laws in the 1950s that allowed blacks and whites to study together in schools and serve together in the military, racism still ruled especially, but not exclusively, in the South. While laws might prevent segregated action, only love could truly reconcile the races. King was convinced of this, which is why "agape" was a key theme in his communication to all audiences. Racial inequality and violence persisted even in places supposedly integrated.

Only someone who could appeal to whites on behalf of blacks, or to blacks on behalf of whites, could reconcile the races. King was well suited to the task. His ecclesiastical and educational experiences were powerful forces that equipped him for the unique role of seeking liberty and justice for all through leadership of the civil rights movement. He accepted this role as his pastoral vocation and civic duty. It cost him his life at age thirty-nine.

Empathy

King's preaching encompassed the emotional and rational, biblical and cultural, common and educated, oppressed and privileged, poor and rich, black and white, and friend and foe. The audience and occasion dictated where he landed on each pole. This dexterity was not attributable to manipulative duplicity[25] or mere rhetorical ability, but to King's empathy. *Time* magazine recognized this when naming King "Man of the Year" in 1964, citing his "indescribable capacity for empathy that is the touchstone of leadership."[26] Richard Lischer, professor emeritus of preaching at Duke

Divinity School, notes "no one could create empathy with audiences as King did."[27] King empathized with black and white audiences in ways that began to move them toward empathy with each other. A critic who once observed the preaching of King admitted he "has an intimate knowledge of the people he is addressing, be they black or white, and in the forthrightness with which he speaks of those things that hurt and baffle them."[28]

Clearly, King's empathic connection with African Americans got the civil rights ball rolling with momentum. He found a way to voice for voiceless blacks their deepest longings. Although King wasn't raised in the urban ghetto, he came across in speech as if he intimately knew the plight of those who were. Some would give credit here to his rhetorical cleverness, but there is more to it. King spent time with all sorts of people who were stuck under the "iron feet of oppression." He listened to, learned from, and cared for them. "Unlike so many talented preachers, he understood the linkage between prophetic vision and the pastoral care of oppressed people."[29]

In a sermon titled "The Prodigal Son," preached to a black congregation at Ebenezer Baptist Church in 1966, King finds a way to empathize with both the national and personal concerns of the congregation. King goes on a litany comparing "beautiful America" to the prodigal son of Luke 15 who left home for a distant country. He says to America, on behalf of his audience, "You went to a tragic far country. A far country of racism where even until this day, America, you leave twenty-two million of your black brothers and sisters living outside of the sunlight of opportunity... you leave twenty-two million of your black brothers humiliated, segregated, dominated politically. America, whenever you stray away from home a famine breaks out."[30]

King continues to be a voice for the voiceless in this sermon, moving seamlessly from their national struggles to personal ones. "I don't know your far country. It may be a bad temper. He's saying you ought to come home this morning. It may be excessive drink... something deep down that causes you to be jealous of people... a family program where you haven't been quite true to your wife or to your husband... you haven't given the attention that you should give to your children, but he's saying to you, you ought to come home this morning."

Of course, King could empathically connect with oppressed African Americans, since he himself was one of them. What makes him such a stellar exemplar of empathic preaching, however, was his ability to connect with white listeners and move them toward empathy for the black community. Empathy is contagious. When addressing white audiences, he used the plural pronouns *we* and *us*. To the mixed crowd of 250,000 who heard the "I Have a Dream" speech, he chose language that was inclusive of a diversity of listeners, including whites. "And when we let freedom ring...we will be able to speed up the day when all of God's children, black men and white men, Jews and gentiles, Protestants and Catholics, will be able to join hands and sing...."[31] King included rural poor whites in his dream declaring to a black congregation at Ebenezer Baptist Church, "I still have a dream today that one day the idle industries of Appalachia will be revitalized."[32] King's empathy moved people on both sides of the fence toward the empathy needed for racial reconciliation.

King not only connected empathically with white listeners and challenged them toward empathy with the black community, he also called black listeners to empathize with whites. In sermons to African American congregations, he called Caucasians "our white brothers." In his message "Antidote to Fear," King invites the black community to empathically love whites: "Once a helpless child, the Negro has now grown politically, culturally, and economically. Many white men fear retaliation. The Negro must show them they have nothing to fear, for the Negro forgives and is willing to forget the past. The Negro must convince the white man that he seeks justice for both himself and the white man."[33]

When white listeners hear a black person preach and feel as if "this preacher gets me," empathic connection is made. Empathy was the primary reason why a black preacher from Georgia rose to such widespread media popularity. "The print and television media had seized upon the oddity of a black man who could articulate the white man's philosophy in a black man's voice."[34] King had a knack for empathy toward all kinds of folks of all different strokes.

King addressed white civic groups and black congregations. He preached in the North and the South, at the Lincoln Memorial in Washington and the Ebenezer Baptist Church in Atlanta. King empathically related to a diversity of groups and moved them, albeit incrementally at times, to empathize with each other. Empathy, then, was the hinge pin on which the door of the civil rights movement swung.

King's Practices

King was a "master adapter"[35] to any preaching context in which he found himself. But what specific homiletic practices enabled his empathic adjustments? There is much to be gleaned from the way King practiced contextuality, collectivity, conversations, courage, and commitment in his preaching ministry.

Contextual. King's contextual preaching was second to none. When preaching to a black congregation, he engaged in empathic hermeneutics. He read and interpreted biblical texts and themes not through the lens of his liberal education and its historical-critical approach to scripture, but through the lens of the African American experience.[36] Instead of debating the authorship or dating of the book of Exodus, for example, he put his black listeners in the sandals of the oppressed Hebrews so that the former could experience the liberation hope of the latter. He also used contextual colloquialisms with black congregations. "I was neck-id in the cold, and I was in prison and you weren't concerned about me, so get out of my face!"[37]

King was contextual when speaking to white or mixed-race audiences too. He left out of these sermons the classic African American rhetorical devices like the movement toward "ecstatic climax"[38] and "the first-person dramatic testimony that places the preacher on the scene of revelation."[39] He frequently repeated sermons but always made contextual adjustments to the content and delivery based on who was listening.

Collective. The use of *collective* language added an empathic tone to King's communication. He used *we, us,* and *ours*[40] whether he was addressing African Americans or Caucasians, clergy or laity, Christian or agnostic. He used affectionate familial language such as "our white brothers" and "my black sisters." Angry or apathetic preachers use *you* as a common pronoun and come across condescendingly as one *above* the listeners. Empathic preachers naturally use collective language and communicate with authenticity, as one *among* the listeners; they garner a hearing from diverse people.

Conversation. King's ability to bond with diverse groups is attributable to his willingness to spend time in conversation with people not like him in terms of ethnicity, education, economics, or spirituality. Educational environments gave him the space to read and converse with a wide range of people. That exposure heightened his empathy for moderate white people. He was part of an interracial council during his college years, which led him to confess, "I had been ready to resent the whole white race, but as I got to see more white people my resentment was softened and a spirit of cooperation took its place."[41]

It's so easy to misunderstand or, worse, demonize people with whom we have little in common. King shows us that the key to empathy is spending time with an assortment of people. When we sit with people to converse over coffee, a meal, or a shared interest with a hospitable and humble posture, we naturally begin to discern how they feel and what they think. Empathy softens resentment and reduces prejudice.

Courage. Christian preaching demands courage; it's not for cowards. King knew this. Empathy and courage seem like an odd couple. However, empathy is the impetus for the kind of courage that enables one to speak the truth in love. While King's empathy attracted diverse people to him and his cause of justice and freedom for all, he received numerous death threats and was eventually murdered at the age of thirty-nine. He was hated by whites who thought he was too black and criticized by blacks who thought he was not black enough. Yet, he kept imploring blacks to empathize with their white brothers and sisters. And he courageously challenged whites to consider their role in supporting injustice and, hopefully, abolishing it. Christian preaching takes courage because it lovingly confronts listeners with hard truth, calling them to embody winsome grace.

Commitment. One final noteworthy preaching practice of King was his commitment. The civil rights movement kept King busy. He traveled and spoke extensively. He dealt with intense political negotiations, threats to his family, and jail. He dealt with fatigue[42] and, some have suggested, "mounting depression"[43] during his later years. Instead of cancelling his preaching commitment on Sundays at Ebenezer Baptist Church, he kept it. "King apparently subscribed to the theory that it is the preacher's job to show up on Sunday morning, no matter what."[44] That level of commitment is born out of empathy and *agape* for the people to whom King preached. It inspires preachers today to aspire to that "mountaintop" of unwavering commitment.

Conclusion: Common Threads in the Preaching of Wesley and King

There are several other notable empathic preachers in church history we could have explored. Phoebe Palmer, Harry Emerson Fosdick, and Aimee Semple McPherson are a few of the exemplars worthy of further consideration. Each of them found a way to preach with empathy in contexts that didn't always, or often, appreciate their empathic orientation. And, of course, Wesley and King experienced lots of exclusion and persecution themselves.

They Inspired Movements

The empathic preaching of John Wesley and Martin Luther King Jr. had some remarkable common characteristics. For starters, their preaching inspired movements. Wesley advanced the Methodist movement and King the civil rights movement. Both of these movements profoundly transformed people, communities, and nations.

They Were Optimistic

Theological anthropology, a capacity to see humanity's potential through the lens of God's promise, drove their empathic preaching. Wesley possessed an "optimism of grace," a belief that depraved human beings can be restored to the *imago Dei* by the work of the Holy Spirit.[45] King similarly believed that the image of God, though tainted, marked the oppressor and oppressed. To King, humans were depraved but not beyond the possibility of racial reconciliation.[46] He was convinced that, to use his words, "there is something in human nature that can respond to goodness...the image of God is never totally gone...the worst segregationist can become an integrationist."[47] Wesley and King preached with joyful hope, believing that God can use something as odd as preaching to perform miracles in human beings, restoring them to what they were before the fall.

They Preached Love

Wesley and King preached on themes that evidence their empathy. The English reformer's sermons hold up "perfect love" as evidence for the sanctification of the human soul. The Baptist preacher from Georgia highlighted "*agape* love" as a prerequisite to liberty and justice for all. They thought often about love, and this, no doubt, significantly enlarged their empathic heart for people.

They Connected across Cultures

Empathic preaching enabled them to bond with people on "the other side of the tracks." The highly educated and churched, prim and proper Wesley preached fruitfully in the fields to the poor, drunk, uneducated, and unchurched people of England, Scotland, Wales, and Ireland. King, a black Baptist preacher, persuaded moderate whites to join his cause. Empathy erased the situational divide between these preachers and their audiences.

Their Published Sermons Were Decontextualized

Admittedly, empathy is not always apparent in their *published* sermons. Wesley's printed sermons were edited for circulation as the concise doctrinal core on which Methodists were formed and their lay preachers preached.[48] The anecdotes and passionate enthusiasm for which Wesley's preaching was known, and sometimes criticized, are largely absent in the published sermons. The printed sermons of King are problematic for similar reasons. King's *Strength to Love* contains sermons and speeches primarily on the topics of racial equality and reconciliation. These sermons were edited for generic appeal and, therefore, suffer the fate of being decontextualized.[49] The good news is that many of King's sermons and speeches have been recorded in their original context and can be accessed today.

Their Preaching Was Costly

The preaching of these empathic exemplars was costly. Wesley describes the many hardships of field-preaching. He traveled on horseback in all kinds of extreme weather, enduring the "summer sun," "wintry rain and wind," "snow like wool," and "hoar-frost like ashes." He called these "the smallest inconveniences." "Far beyond all these," he wrote, were the "contempt and reproach of every kind ... verbal affronts, stupid, brutal violence, sometimes to the hazard of health, or limbs, or life."[50]

King describes the cost of empathic preaching: "I've been in more than 18 jail cells.... I've come perilously close to death at the hands of a demented Negro woman.... I've seen my home bombed three times.... I've had to live every day under the threat of death."[51] A commitment to empathy killed preacher King. He was shot dead on the evening of April 4, 1968.

Christological suffering was the theological lens through which Wesley and King understood their ministries. Their identification with Christ was not the result of spiritual pride but was rooted in the joy of empathic union with the suffering servant. That alone kept their empathic preaching going when the going got tough.

Part III: Framing the House

Practices for Cultivating Empathy in Preachers

Introduction: Can Your Empathy Grow?

The preacher must become a person of empathy in the quest to preach with empathy. Trying to preach with empathy before practicing empathy is putting the ministry cart before the spiritual horse. Preaching with empathy is more of a spiritual art than a rhetorical skill. Real empathy is fluid and organic, not static and contrived. The good news is that while empathy cannot be forced or faked, it can be cultivated through intentional and consistent practices.

If you are tempted to conclude, "empathy is not my strong suit; it's not my spiritual gift and I'm too set in my ways to change," hold on! You can grow your empathic muscles. According to empathy authority Roman Krznaric, "there is overwhelming agreement among the experts that our personal empathy quota is not fixed" and that "we can develop our empathic potential throughout our lives."[1]

Christian discipleship is a process of learning to empathize with the God who empathizes with us, learning to love what God loves (i.e., people) and hate what God hates (i.e., injustice). If this is true, and I'm convinced it is, then surely the Holy Spirit can restore our empathic wiring. God tends to restore us through spiritual disciplines, practices that over time become virtue-forming dispositions and habits. The practices in this chapter can potentially expand your empathy quotient beyond its current sum. They are essentially spiritual disciplines intended to form "Christ living in you, the hope of glory."[2] Before we consider some empathy-cultivating practices, let's reflect briefly on empathy's barriers and benefits.

Barriers and Benefits of Empathy in the Preacher

There are barriers to empathy in the preacher. Shame, guilt, insecurity, and inferiority along with egotism and arrogance can block the empathy necessary for intimacy with God and people. Perhaps the greatest barrier to empathy for preachers is the fear of vulnerability. Brené Brown, *New York Times* bestselling author, writes, "The level to which we protect ourselves from being vulnerable is a measure of our fear and disconnection...we must dare to show up and let ourselves be seen."[3] Let's face it, taking off the clerical robe is risky. People will inevitably see our wrinkles and warts. However, "empathic relationships cannot easily develop unless we reveal ourselves and seek connection."[4] Relationships are well worth the risk of vulnerability, especially for pastors who are all too often lonely and isolated from the very communities they serve.

Those who access the divine grace necessary to break through the barriers experience life-giving benefits. Empathy growth will enhance just about every area of the preacher's life—friendship, marriage, parenting, ministry, and health. To put it bluntly, the people around you will like you more when you love them empathically. It would be worthwhile to consider how an increase in empathy positively impacts every relational arena. However, a focused reflection on how empathy benefits the ministry and health of the preacher is most applicable here.

Cultural

Diversity is a reality everywhere, even in my small midwestern suburban neighborhood. On my block alone, consisting of about twenty-five homes, there are African American, Asian, Caucasian, East Indian, Filipino, Haitian, Latino, Native American, and Russian neighbors. I suspect that English is a second language for some of them. Globalization used to be digital, but in many places it is physical. The world lives on my street.

Some lament this diversity, seeing it as a threat. Others, with vision, see it as a golden opportunity for the church to "do" global missions locally and to learn what other cultures have to offer us. The give-and-take is reciprocal. There have been excellent books written to resource pastors seeking to foster multiethnic and multicultural congregations.[5] Empathic pastors envision a diverse congregation as a beautiful reflection of our trinitarian God. Pastoral and congregational empathy for "the other," embodied in the Trinity from eternity, is the premier tool enabling the church to seize the opportunity presented by diversity. Empathy makes cross-cultural ministry not only possible but probable. Only when we empathically take the perspective of diverse people, understanding their thoughts and feelings, can we authentically "become all things to all people."[6]

Congregational

A major benefit of empathy in the preacher is what it does, in time, to the congregation. Through sermon after sermon, week after week, preachers call people to live into the gospel of Jesus Christ. Many of us who preach frequently proclaim the importance of loving people inside and outside of the church. We tell heartwarming chicken-soup-for-the-soul stories designed to inspire our people toward reconciliation with God, family, friends, and, if we're brave, enemies. But the most compelling inspiration comes from the preacher's life within and beyond the preaching event. Empathy demonstrated by the preacher is contagious to the congregation. Your growth in empathy probably won't positively infect all people, but it will impact some and maybe many. And, as is the case with the word that we plant, the effect is accumulative; it builds over time.

Pastors want their congregants to be a little nicer. The best way to promote empathic kindness is to live it as we proclaim it. Psychologist Alan Sroufe advises, "you get an empathic child by being empathic with the child."[7] Empathic congregations are cultivated by empathic pastors.

Clerical

The preaching life is joy-filled but emotionally, spiritually, and physically rigorous. There's no escaping this double-edged homiletic sword. It cuts both ways. When preachers experience more rigor than joy for a prolonged period, they burn out. The exhausted preacher robotically goes through the motions of developing and delivering sermons. Preaching becomes a task done *for* instead of *with* God and the church. On the other hand, preachers who maintain their empathic connection to God and to people while engaged in the rigors of the homiletic process are likely to experience an increase in joy and a lengthy ministry tenure.

In this chapter and the next, you will encounter dozens of practices aimed at cultivating empathy in preachers and infusing empathy in preaching. The goal is not to overwhelm you with more tasks than you have now or to make the homiletic process more exhausting than it is already. Instead, I hope these ideas will liberate you to modify your process in ways that heighten your intimacy with God and your congregation, enhancing your joy in preaching.

Practices

This chapter is loaded with practices—spiritual disciplines—designed to help you become a more empathic person in ministry and beyond, toward your spouse, your children, friends, strangers, and enemies. Start an electronic or hard copy "Empathy Journal" to record observations, insights, and questions that you glean from the empathic experiments below. You may want to try one or two practices each week. After you test-drive each, decide which ones to employ on a regular basis in your quest to become a more empathic person and preacher.

Incarnational Immersion

There are plenty of TV shows about swapping. There is *Trading Spaces* and *Wife Swap*, but my favorite is BBC's *The Life Swap Adventure*. Two people from opposite worlds, like a rural farmer and an urban taxi driver or a bull rider and a pony polo player, trade lives for a few weeks. People step out of their lives to take on the perspective of a person who is not like them.

John Howard Griffin did something like this in the racially segregated South of the 1950s. Griffin, a white man, made his skin black for six weeks to experience what it might be like to be an African American male. He immersed himself in the black experience and then wrote about it in order to expose racial discrimination.[8] His empathic concern for black men soared. Immersion is an effective method for developing empathy.

Of course, most of us can't leave behind our lives, our relationships and responsibilities, to take on someone else's for a couple of weeks. But there are creative ways to incarnationally immerse ourselves into the shoes of other people so that we increase our empathic understanding of them.

God incarnationally immersed Godself into human reality when, through Christ, God came onto our turf to become one of us and one with us. Essentially, God swapped God's life for ours. We certainly got the better end of that trade.

Perhaps once each week, try to experience life from another's perspective. Spend eight hours blindfolded (and not just while you sleep!) to help you imagine what life is like without sight. Sit all day or sleep at night in a park without food, drink, or conversation to feel the hunger, cold, shame, and loneliness of the homeless. Go to your local McDonald's a few consecutive mornings from eight to ten a.m. to observe how senior citizens interact. Plop down on a barstool midday or late at night to watch and engage people numbing their pain. Try to live on one dollar per day for a week to experience, in small measure, what it might be like to be poor. Spend an hour walking the halls of a nursing home to feel for and with people who have lost some basic human capacities.

The point is that we need to resist the gravitational pull to stay locked away in an office or study, writing sermons in quarantine from the sorts of people we hope our preaching will liberate and empower in some way. The preacher who wants to grow in empathy is wise to go out and see where people study, work, play, hurt, heal, and "live and move and have [their] being." What one sees impacts what one feels.[10] If we are going to feel for and with others, it helps to see them in their contexts.

Watching people in pain, though exhausting, is an effective empathy-inducer. I had some excellent courses in homiletics during my educational journey. The best preaching course I ever had, however, was not a preaching course at all. During my seminary days, I was required to serve in a parachurch ministry for one semester. I fulfilled this requirement by serving as a hospice chaplain. Several times each week I would sit with people in physical, emotional, and, quite often, spiritual pain. I visited a forty-year-old mother of three small boys who was dying of pancreatic cancer. I read Psalms to a man in his sixties who had no visits from family as he battled liver cirrhosis caused by alcohol. The learning curve was steep that semester. I learned so much I didn't know about God, myself, and all kinds of people. Immersion in the lives of people in pain made me a more empathic preacher.

Telling the Truth

We all have aversions. I dislike vinegar, my teenage son's odor after basketball practice, most political news reporting, and the Dallas Cowboys, to name a few. Let's be honest, many of us have a distaste for certain people or groups. One of the fiercely challenging but best practices for developing our empathic muscles is learning to take the cognitive and affective perspective of people we don't like, our enemies even. Roman Krznaric said, "Empathy with 'the enemy' can play a crucial healing role and resolve the deadlocks that beset our relationships."[11] Jesus knew this, so he challenged his followers with "love your enemies."[12]

The first step toward enemy-empathy is to admit your aversion. In your "Empathy Journal," respond to the following progression of questions: Which person or group is the biggest empathy barrier for you? What specifically don't you like or disagree with about that person or group? What does this reveal about you, in terms of your convictions, wounds, prejudices, hopes, past, and preferences? Borrowing from Fred Craddock, imagine "what it's like to be" the person or group with whom you struggle. This imaginative act can "keep alive and functioning a minister's empathetic understanding."[13] Record this imaginative reflection in your journal. In fact, you might even extend this journal exercise to include a small group in your congregation. Find ways to help people grow with you in empathy.

Doing this exercise will not necessarily cause you to like someone you dislike, but it might help you to love them empathetically. It can happen. A Ku Klux Klan leader and African American civil rights leader do become friends.[14] A woman reconciles with the IRA bomber who killed her father. Together they travel around the world to speak about empathy and reconciliation.[15] Maybe it doesn't happen often enough, but empathic miracles do occur. Perhaps someday I just might learn to love the Dallas Cowboys professional football team. Nah.

Booking

Harriet Beecher Stowe was born in 1811 and had a privileged upbringing that included black servants. In 1852, Stowe wrote *Uncle Tom's Cabin*, a powerful story that empathically connected white readers to the harsh realities of black slaves. The book sold four million copies within ten years. In the midst of the Civil War, President Lincoln purportedly said upon meeting Stowe, "So you're the little woman who wrote the book that started this great war." Preachers of the Bible should have no problem believing that God can use something as common as a book to move people from revelation to resolution, and finally, to revolution.

Reading books by or about people with whom we already resonate may be pleasurable, but it does little to expand our empathy quotient. Instead, read books that help you understand the mind and emotions of people not like you. The goal is not necessarily to endorse or agree with people who think or live differently than you; the aim is empathic understanding.

So, if you are a staunch Republican, read the autobiographies of Barack Obama and Hillary Clinton. If you are a devout Democrat, read the life stories of Condoleezza Rice and George W. Bush. Read people with different theological views than the ones you hold. Check out classic and contemporary literary works that feature a protagonist that is not like you in terms of gender, age, ethnicity, education, and/or religion. If you are a white male in your forties like me, consider reading *I Know Why the Caged Bird Sings* by Maya Angelou, an African American woman writing about the pain and hope of her adolescent years.

Go and grab a few books from your local library that are written by or about a person with whom you have little in common. The online *Empathy Library*[16] can steer you in the right direction. Mix in biographies and autobiographies with classic and contemporary fiction. Then start booking! The goal, again, is not agreement or endorsement but empathy. Start a book club and invite others to join you.

Viewing

"Looking at pictures almost certainly contributes to the development and refinement" of empathic skills.[17] This is why billions of dollars are expended to produce and present images (photographs, graphics, commercials, sitcoms, movies) that change perceptions and create empathic bonds. Movies, especially, are "empathy machines."[18] Film critic Roger Ebert said, "Movies are like a machine that generates empathy. It lets you understand a little bit more about different hopes, aspirations, dreams, and fears."[19]

Not long ago, I watched the 2016 film *Moonlight*. I didn't have much of an idea what the film was about, but knew enough to suspect it might broaden my empathic horizons. It did. I wondered as I watched the movie how someone like me, a white, heterosexual, well-educated, middle-aged, northeastern, Christian minister could empathically bond with the central character, a young, African American, uneducated, homosexual drug dealer from Miami. It didn't take long for me to identify a significant common thread with that character. The little we shared was enough to create a connection that caused me to cry empathic tears like a baby for most of the movie. Despite our obvious dissimilarities, our common points of pain built an empathic bridge that surprised me. Excellent films with round, not flat, character development and a profound plot do this so well.

Gandhi, Schindler's List, Philadelphia, A Time to Kill, The Elephant Man, and *The Hunchback of Notre Dame* are just a few of the films that have empathy-cultivating potential. A quick Google search for "movies that inspire empathy" should produce good results. If you get stuck, go to the *Empathy Library* website.[20] The site has concise, helpful descriptions about each film.

Instead of watching the films alone, start your own little Empathy Film Club. You can gather with your spouse and kids, with church staff, and/or with friends. After you view the film, consider discussing the following questions: In what ways did you empathically connect with the central character? What hopes or hurts do you have in common with the central character? What character elicited the least empathy from you and why? If you view the film alone, articulate your response to these questions in your "Empathy Journal."

Ethnographic Interviews

Jesus said in John 10:14, "I am the good shepherd. I know my own sheep." One of the ways pastoral shepherds come to know their flock is through ethnographic study. The ethnographer "goes into a culture, establishes rapport with its inhabitants, and analyzes the culture while also becoming immersed in its day-to-day activities."[21] Sounds a lot like pastoral ministry.

Analyze your congregation through the lenses of ethnicity, generation, economics, and education. Imagine that a guest preacher is coming to preach at your church and asks you to describe your flock.[22]

What ethnic groups are represented in your congregation? What is the largest and the smallest? What ethnic groups are increasing and decreasing most? Do the ethnic trends in the church match those in the community?

What generations are represented in your congregation? What is the largest and smallest age group: 0–20, 21–40, 41–60, 61–80? What age groups are increasing and decreasing most?

What economic levels are present in your congregation? What is the largest and the smallest group: lower, middle, or upper? What levels are increasing or decreasing most?

What education levels are represented in your congregation (primary, secondary, undergraduate, graduate, doctorate)? What education levels are most and least represented? What levels are growing or declining most?

Write a demographic description of your congregation responding to the questions above. Use your "Empathy Journal." Of course, demographics alone could never fully capture the identity of your congregation; it's only a start.

Now it's time to dig deeper by conducting ethnographic interviews. Think of the people in each demographic category (ethnicity, generation, economics, education) with whom you have the least in common or the hardest time connecting. For example, you may be a thirty-year-old pastor who struggles to connect with congregants in their sixties. Or maybe you have an undergraduate degree and can't relate to people with doctorates. Meet one-on-one for coffee with the four individuals who are most different from you ethnically, generationally, economically, or educationally. First, get to know their story by inquiring with genuine interest about their upbringing, career, discipleship journey, marriage, and family. Then, ask them pointed questions that will probe their preaching preferences. What do you think makes good preaching good and bad preaching bad? What are the preaching needs of people in your demographic subgroup? How does the preaching at our church meet or not meet those needs?

Scott Hoezee, in *Actuality: Real Life Stories for Sermons That Matter*, connects a sociological research method called *visual ethnography* with preaching. He invites preachers to consider giving cheap disposable cameras to people in the congregation to take pictures of their lives in action. Perhaps the four congregants in your ethnographic study can take snapshots of their lives at work, at home, at school, while traveling, and elsewhere and give them to you "as a way to gain a virtual window into the lives of the very people"[23] to whom you preach.

The demographic description coupled with the four interviews and visuals will move you closer toward saying with Jesus, "I know my sheep." When you finish each interview, journal an empathic prayer for the interviewee and the subgroup they represent in your congregation. Preaching with empathy entails doing whatever it takes to speak from and into the lives of people from all subgroups without alienating anyone.

The Breakfast Club

If you were a teenager in the 1980s, you probably saw *The Breakfast Club*. The movie features five high-schoolers from very different walks of life who are forced together by Saturday detention. Their prejudices toward each other surface quickly. Throughout the long day of detention, they each tell their story and reveal their struggles. Despite the differences between them, these teenagers begin to bond around the common pain of the human condition. This film presents a powerful picture of empathy. Plus it has some nice 80s music too.

Establish your own breakfast club. Identify four people in your congregation who come from different walks of life than you and each other. If possible, include both genders, various generations, and multiple ethnicities. Of course, these are not the only markers of difference. You might also consider spiritual diversity. Bring together the seasoned saint with the new believer or agnostic seeker in your church. It might be dangerous, but give people with divergent political affiliations a seat in your breakfast club. Basically, imagine four people in your congregation who seem so different from each other that you would never want them in a small group together. Ever! That's the perfect breakfast club!

The breakfast club should meet for breakfast, of course, monthly for six to twelve months. After that, you can select a new group. Pick a monthly day, time, and place that works for everyone in the group and try to stick with it. The first meeting of your breakfast club might consist of simple introductions and small talk. In the meetings that follow, you'll want to guide the group toward deeper discussion. After a few meetings, you can rotate the role of discussion facilitator so you're not always the one leading.

When it comes to discussion topics, nothing is off limits. You might want to create for participants an actual conversation menu with a bunch of questions from which they can choose to respond. Explore topics that are usually off limits, such as politics and religion. Invite participants to share their opinions about abortion and gun control. Ask them to weigh in on current events discussed in the news. We all know these kinds of conversations can go off the rails quickly and destroy a group. Because of this, take extra time in the first meeting to talk about group ground rules and goals. If you clearly state that the goal of the group is to learn to empathize with people not like you, it can alleviate some of the risk.

Take turns sharing a recent high and low or, as some call it, "a happy and a crappy." As the group begins to empathically bond together, like the teenagers in *The Breakfast Club*, a more mature level of sharing about past hurts and future hopes will likely occur. The goal is to replace judgment, prejudice, and stereotyping with genuine empathic concern. Be sure to record questions, observations, and insights in your "Empathy Journal."

Social Media as a Spiritual Discipline

Krznaric laments, "There is mounting evidence that the digital revolution... is failing to send us on the path toward an empathic civilization."[25]

It's hard to argue with his suspicion regarding social media and other technologies. After a scroll through Facebook or e-news sites, I'm ready for a shower to wash off the filth. Seriously, even casual engagement with social media can leave us feeling angry, hopeless, jealous, inferior, self-righteous, desperate, narcissistic, or judgmental. I wonder about the destructive impact of social media upon divorce, violence, racism, and depression. Would the world be better off without social media?

I'm not ready to throw out the technological baby with the dirty bath water. God has always found a means to inhabit our way of life. In an ancient world that revolved around religious cultic practices and law, God established a sacrificial system and the Ten Commandments to govern people. To reach first-century Jews, God came to the world as a first-century Jew named Jesus. As God comes to us through the ordinary bread and wine of the Eucharist, so God comes to us through the ordinary, day-to-day realities of the world we inhabit. Social media is where we live. Surely God can redeem it.

What if we engage social media in ways that foster empathy? Maybe social media can function like a spiritual discipline. I'm convinced that while social media can certainly oppress and depress, it can also be a premier tool God uses to increase our empathy for the world God created and loves.

Let's explore a few of the many ways we can engage social mediums like Facebook, Instagram, and Twitter as empathically formative disciplines. As more and more followers of Christ practice the ideas below, social media will become redemptive. Here are some social media practices that are more formational than deformational.

Take a prayer scroll. Scroll through your Facebook feed prayerfully. Read the posts of friends and family members slowly, trying to discern the dreams and disappointments behind their words. Ask God to give you intercessory empathy. Then, pray for people as led by God's spirit. If you come across a shared story from a news network about racial violence, a natural disaster, political shaming, or some other painful situation, pray empathically for God's intervention. Try to imagine the feelings and thoughts of the people or groups for whom you will pray. Before you post, like, or share, pray. Start your day with a ten- to fifteen-minute empathic prayer scroll.

Celebrate others. Let's be honest, our social media posts are veiled (barely) attempts to show people our wisdom, accomplishments, cute kids, wonderful spouse, home décor, healthy diet, or exercise results. Of course, this is not an entirely egotistical use of social media. We should share the good stuff going on in our lives with family and friends. But what if we focused more on empathically highlighting the wisdom and achievements of others than showcasing our own? It would drastically change social media. I have a friend who uses social media exclusively to celebrate others. He empathically follows the counsel of Paul by "rejoic[ing] with those who rejoice."[26] It seems easier to "weep with those who weep" than to "rejoice with those who rejoice." Let's empathically celebrate others, as if their joy is ours. The next time you are on Facebook, celebrate someone else by liking, sharing, or commending their post. When you open Twitter, retweet someone else's profound statement, book announcement, or thoughtful article. Or simply post or tweet a few words to celebrate, endorse, or empower some person or group. Try to celebrate others via social media at least seven times daily for seven days.

Speak for the voiceless. Social media is full of rants, which is why some of us take a periodic sabbatical from it. But the negative, even abusive ranting is no reason for us to miss out on using social media to empathically speak up for those who can't, won't, or don't speak up for themselves. In order to get a hearing in a sea of ranting, we will need to expose injustice in thoughtful, gracious, forthright, and loving ways. Jesus came from the father "full of grace and truth" (John 1:14). Grace and truth are good guidelines for social media engagement. Be a voice for the people for whom Jesus was a voice. Post or tweet something that exposes the plight of the poor, mentally ill, persecuted, or socially ostracized. Expose the ugliness of human trafficking and drug addiction, as well as policies and systems that marginalize people. Be a voice of empathy for the voiceless once or twice daily via all of your social media accounts. Invite your Facebook friends and Twitter followers to do the same.

Consistent Communion

Call it what you like—Communion, the Lord's Supper, or the Eucharist—but take it frequently. I've been a part of a congregation that participated in the Eucharist weekly and a member of another that took Communion quarterly or less. I admit there are thoughtful reasons for taking the sacrament infrequently, but I find myself needing this means of grace more not less as I grow older.

Maybe I'm a Protestant mystic, but it seems that something supernaturally unexplainable happens when we open our mouths and lives to Christ's body and blood, the bread and wine. Regardless of what we believe about the elements, most Christian traditions agree that God, by grace, enters into us more fully as we partake. And, since Christ is the empathic king of kings and lord of lords, receiving him through the bread and cup makes us more mystically empathic too.

It's important to note here the importance of empathic communion with the people in our local Christian community. Paul warned the Corinthian congregation about making the sacrament of Communion an occasion for the rich to divide from the poor. The rich had the luxury of not working a full day or at all, while the poor worked long hours. The rich consumed the elements before the poor arrived at worship. There is interpretive debate regarding 1 Corinthians 11:17-34. Was it a potluck supper or the Lord's Supper the apostle was talking about? At any rate, Paul's point is clear. "When you gather to eat, you should all eat together."[27] Paul is challenging, even commanding, the Corinthian congregation back then and, by extension, the church today to embody in our relationships with others the empathy of the one whose body was broken and blood shed for us. The Eucharist, then, is a grace that invites and inculcates both vertical and horizontal empathic dimensions. Through the sacrament, congregants encounter God as "empathy expressed through the incarnation of Christ."[28] Eat and sip often.

Marginal Ministry

From a distance, empathy is hard to muster. Empathy is best cultivated in us through engagement that is up close and personal, face-to-face, and life-to-life. Norm was a crotchety guy in his seventies who attended the church I served as pastor. He sat in the service with a frown and crossed arms. He had been a Christian for decades but was spiritually dry and emotionally constipated (sorry for the imagery). Sunday school class, small group, and congregational worship, while they didn't hurt Norm, didn't seem to help him out of the wilderness.

By accident, Norm bumped into a group of homeless people who started to gather at the hardware store. At first, he was bothered by their loitering. Then, he was introduced to a few of them by the owner of the store. Norm began sipping coffee with his homeless friends. Soon, he was bringing them to his home and church. One fall, with the harsh Northeast winter coming, he gathered a bunch of guys from the church to build shelters in the woods where his homeless friends lived. He paid for materials, recruited the labor, and got the job done.

Norm experienced resurrection. What did it? God orchestrated Norm's empathic connection to people on the margins. Norm came to life.

People on the margins are enduring life with basic needs unmet. They live without food, clothing, shelter, relationships, health, freedom, hope, or love. So many of us get stuck behind a desk, keeping all balls in the air the best we can. Let them drop. Go spend time with people on the margins monthly, maybe weekly. Visit people in prisons, nursing homes, addiction rehabs, orphanages, homeless shelters, and hospitals. Spend time with shut-ins, immigrants, and widows. We don't necessarily need a mission trip to a third-world country to encounter marginalized people. They are all around us.

Ministry to people on the margins is more about offering friendship than charity. Christine Pohl makes the case that people on the societal fringes need "a safe, personal, and comfortable place...of respect and acceptance and friendship."[29] Empathy may start with charity, but it ends in relationship, the ultimate goal of empathy.

Empathic Hospitality

Jesus was known, and critiqued, for eating with people not like him, namely "tax collectors and sinners."[30] For "sinners," read "prostitutes." Jesus exemplified hospitable openness to a diversity of people. He ate with people who didn't look like, think like, believe like, or act like him. And, according to 1 John 4:17b, "In this world we are like Jesus" (NIV).

The empathic practice I'm going to propose is likely the most challenging but also the most rewarding. Think of four to six people from your neighborhood, workplace, school, church, or team who are not like you in some major way. Identify as many people as possible in your social network who are different from you in several of the following areas: spiritually, ethnically, politically, economically, generationally, or educationally. Circle the names of people who are least like you. Pick four to six of them to invite to your house this month for dinner. Maybe you will want to have this group back again in a couple of months. They might even invite you to their place for a meal. This practice can heighten your capacity to empathically imagine what it is like to be Buddhist, or Japanese, or Republican, or poor, or eighty, or a PhD. Christians, of all people, know full well that something extraordinary can happen around a table where food is served.

Empathy Detective

I tend to struggle with mild depression during the presidential election season; call it seasonal depression. This past presidential election was no different. Unfortunately, more than a few people can relate. The venomous speeches and commercials can chip away at the most joyful of people.

One way I combated the negative words and images entering my brain was by becoming an empathy detective. I was on the prowl for empathy in action. When I saw empathy in the restaurant, workplace, neighborhood, gym, traffic, movie, or news, I recorded it in my little black book (it's red actually). Seeking and finding empathic good in people offset my sadness.

Channel your inner Sherlock Holmes by being an empathy detective. You can take a little notebook with you or take notes on your smartphone when you see empathy in action. Or you can record your empathy-sleuthing results once each day in your "Empathy Journal" while in the comfort of your home or favorite coffee shop. Identification of empathy nurtures imitation of empathy.

Community Connection

If we believe with John Wesley that "the world is [our] parish," we will preach to address not just congregational but community needs. Pastors shepherd not just the people in the church but neighbors in the community around the church. In order to empathize with the community, we have to know the community.

Develop a list of questions that will help you get to know your community. You might include demographic questions that explore trends in the community regarding age, ethnicity, economics, and religion. Census data can help provide some of the answers.

The next step is the most crucial. Make a list of ten to twelve leaders in your community. Focus on people who know and serve the community well. You might include the mayor, service organization directors, school principals, police chiefs, business owners, and politicians. Contact the people on your list and invite each of them to one-on-one coffee, breakfast, or lunch. You buy. They are busy serving the community, so promise not to take more than an hour of their valuable time.

During your meeting with each of these leaders, express appreciation for their service and ask them the following two questions: What do you think are the most pressing needs in our community? What do you think the church can do to meet those needs?

I adopted this practice in the last community I served as pastor. These meetings revealed that racial reconciliation and addiction recovery were two of the most significant community concerns. I began to preach to these needs, and it, coupled with lots of prayer, shaped the identity of our church.

The congregation became more knowledgeable and empathetic regarding these social issues. We started a food pantry, homeless shelter, and various recovery groups for people addicted to drugs, gambling, sex, or alcohol. The church tackled the problem of racism with refreshing sincerity. In a few years, we were known as a community-involved, racially diverse, and addiction-recovery congregation. But it started with empathically caring and praying about the concerns of our community.

The Walmart Walk

Since we're on the topic of community, let's run with it or, better, walk with it. Most communities have a Walmart, or a similar store, that attracts all sorts of people from the surrounding community. Walmart particularly draws into its store people on the margins, living paycheck to paycheck, or welfare check to welfare check.

Take a thirty-minute walk in Walmart weekly not to shop but to cultivate your empathy for people in your community. Maybe you can do this exercise while fasting from breakfast or lunch. Walk up and down the aisles inviting God to give you empathy. Try not to speak at all. Just walk, don't talk. Look deep into the eyes of people coming your way, trying your best not to creep them out with staring. Ask God for empathic discernment into the situations of their lives. Then intercede in prayer for people as led by the Holy Spirit.

I've done this simple exercise with seminary students and pastors at my local Walmart. At first, this practice seems a bit odd, frightening even, to them. When we come back to debrief after the experience, most of them are surprised by how this practice empathically moved them. The empathy of Christ enables them to see and feel the stress, sorrow, regret, insecurity, addiction, hope, joy, peace, anger, inferiority, and shame in peoples' eyes. When they do, their own empathy develops.

Empathic Ecology

I searched "ecological empathy" on the Internet. The first hit was the Superpower Wiki website. Apparently, the ability to feel for and with the environment is a superpower. DC Comics' "Swamp Thing" possesses this talent. Seriously.

You don't have to be a tree-hugging swamp thing with an innate environmental connection to practice ecological empathy. Recall the creation story. Genesis 2:15 tells us that "The Lord God took the man and put him in the Garden of Eden to work it and take care of it" (NIV). Forgive the paraphrase, but God essentially said to Adam, and all of humanity by extension, "Be sure not to exploit but to steward the earth as a gift from me to you." The earth is a gift from God passed down from our ancestors to us and from us to our descendants.

Empathic care for the earth is a command from God that ultimately blesses us and those who come behind us. I hated seeing cups and candy wrappers when I hiked beautiful trails in Maine's Acadia National Park last summer. The mess that other people left behind for me to deal with bugged me. We don't want our descendants to feel as though we left them a mess by not caring for creation.

There are all sorts of ideas for practicing ecological empathy. Here are three. Reduce what you throw away. Trash hurts the environment, plain and simple. Reuse what you can. Perhaps you can repurpose something that has run its course. An old chicken crate is now a piece of furniture in our living room. Recycle what you can. It's amazing to me what is being recycled these days. Not only are paper, cardboard, and glass recyclable; so are batteries, bulbs, and electronics. Get your family and friends to join you in practicing empathic ecology.[31]

Leeching

A leech is a blood-sucking worm that attaches to flesh and is hard to pry loose. Forgive the imagery, but we may need to practice a form of leeching in our quest to be more empathic.

Leech on or, to put it another way, latch on to empathic people in your life. Who are some of the supremely empathic people you know at home, work, school, church, or in the neighborhood? Reflect on the ways they embody empathy toward you and others. Text, e-mail, or message today one of the most empathic people you know to schedule a lunch soon.

Empathy is as contagious as chicken pox but better for you. Spending time with empathic people will do something good to you. Your capacity to empathically imagine yourself in other peoples' shoes so that you think how they think and feel what they feel will escalate. Of course, the opposite is also true. Spending time with apathetic people who lack empathy might stifle your empathic potential.

Conclusion: Baby Steps

Just like a healthy weight-loss program, empathy growth is often incremental. Becoming a more empathic person takes time and lots of baby steps, but it can happen. The cultivation of empathy, however, happens intentionally not accidentally. Like the continual pressure of a flowing stream changes the color and shape of the rock, so the consistent employment of the practices above will transform you over time.

There are so many empathy-cultivating practices in this chapter. Don't attempt to do all of them all of the time. Try one practice each week and see how it goes. After you've had a chance to engage all of them, regularly employ the exercises you think will increase your empathy the most. Maybe you can incorporate some of these practices as New Year's resolutions.

What God does to you, he wants to do through you. Put another way, as you grow in the spiritual grace of empathy, be open to the ways God wants to partner with you to cultivate empathy in your congregation. Empathy is the work of the entire Christian community, not just the pastor. Many of the practices above are designed for groups. Those that are not, can be adapted. Consider inviting your staff, elders, board members, congregants, family, and friends to practice some of these empathic disciplines with you. Spiritual growth is most enjoyable when it happens in the context of community. Be sure to take people with you on your quest to be more empathic. It could transform you, your family, and your church.

Chapter 6

Practices for Infusing Empathy in Preaching

Introduction: Words Create Empathy

The previous chapter listed practices that preachers can engage to become more empathic people. Here we consider practices that help preachers craft more empathic sermons.

Extreme anger and apathy abound. The United States is currently not so united. We are divided along the boundary lines of politics, race, and economics, to name just a few. Misunderstanding, caricaturing, and stereotyping are norms in this allegedly advanced society. The good news is that what we preachers say and how we say it can offset this trend, assuming we preach with empathy in a callous culture.

Words create worlds that shape reality for the speaker and the listener. Kathryn A. Flynn notes that, "Discourse shapes and establishes what will become the social reality within any given context."[1] Flynn asserts that empathic discourse is the way forward in dealing with the "acute social challenges" of our day. Empathic language "embodies compassion, allowance of complexity, and sensitivity to context."[2] What we say and how we say it not only reflects but impacts our level of empathy, not to mention the congregation's. Flynn cautions, "Let us choose then, most carefully, our words."[3]

Choosing "most carefully" our sermonic words demands "faithfulness to the Gospel and fittingness for the congregation."[4] The preacher listens empathically to the heart of God through scripture and to the hopes of humanity in context. Then, like a courier who delivers notes between two lovers, the preacher offers theologically faithful and contextually fitting words to reconcile God and people. This kind of sermon is, like Christ, born with divine and human essence all over it.

This chapter contains practices designed to help the preacher listen to the heart of God and the hopes of humanity in the process of crafting and communicating sermons. Preaching with empathy comes after listening with empathy to God *and* people, to the text *and* the context.

As mentioned, empathic preaching is more of a spiritual and contextual art, than a rhetorical technique. It's more like making pasta sauce than baking brownies. The brownie recipe is regimented. The instructions on the brownie mix tell you what to add and when to add it. Follow the rules with rigidity or else. I'd rather make pasta sauce than bake brownies. Maybe it's my Italian heritage, but I love to come up with my own sauces. I will dice up almost anything in the cupboard and fridge—zucchini, squash, black olives, onions, and tomatoes. I will add a dash of soy sauce, cooking wine, oregano, parsley, Slap Ya Mama Cajun spice, and pepper. After tasting, I will add another dash of this or that, depending on my mood and, most importantly, the tastes of those for whom I'm cooking. Preaching with empathy is more like creatively making sauce than rigidly baking brownies.

The following practices will guide you toward the empathic planning, crafting, delivering, and evaluating of sermons. Experiment with one or two each time you write a sermon. When you've worked through all of the exercises, decide which ones to incorporate regularly in your quest to preach with empathy.

Practices

Give Them God

It's important to establish from the outset of this section that preaching with empathy is as much of a theological enterprise as it is a practical one. Sermons that transform people are not only culturally relevant, they're theologically substantive. No matter how hard preachers try to practice empathy, which is a good idea, God is the one who empowers empathy in the preacher and the listener. G. Lee Ramsey said, "The preacher weaves empathy into the caring language that establishes congregational communion.

None of this ever closes the door on the active participation of God through Christ and the Holy Spirit. Rather, it recognizes that the preacher pastor's ability to establish communion with the hearer is one means whereby God does the work of grace through preaching."[5] If the preacher and congregation have any chance at empathy, God must be central to the preaching act and the sermon content. If not, then the pursuit of empathy turns into a form of moralism based on a "try harder" and "do better" legalism. The preacher is not a therapist or self-help guru but a pastoral theologian who proclaims the triune God and the incarnate Christ to a hope-needy human race. Preachers give people not good advice, but God.

There are several practices to help preachers keep God, the empathy-infuser, central to the sermon. Asking theological questions throughout the sermon-crafting process is crucial to ensuring that the preacher has something to say that's worth saying. Here are vital theological inquiries for the empathic preacher:

- What of substance does the sermon say about the Father, the Son, and/or the Holy Spirit that is true, insightful, and compelling?

- How does this sermon faithfully reflect what the biblical story reveals overall about the empathic God?

- What does God seem to be saying and/or doing through this particular biblical text to cultivate the grace of empathy in his people?

- How does the purpose of the sermon align with the purposes of God made manifest in this text?

- Does the sermon present the gospel by honestly proclaiming both the problem of human sin and the resolution of divine grace?

The preacher who reflects on these questions in the process of developing and delivering sermons will likely have something of theological substance to proclaim.

Homileticians often debate whether or not the sermon should focus on God, Jesus Christ, or any member of the Trinity if the biblical text being preached doesn't explicitly mention them. This important debate is worthy of a detailed response, but here's a practice you might find helpful. It is true that many biblical texts don't name God or Jesus explicitly.

In fact, most do not. Yet, I've already advocated preaching sermons that consistently feature God as the hero and climactic highpoint. Every single biblical text is set within a canonical context in which God figures prominently. The biblical narrative from Genesis to Revelation is the interpretive lens through which every single textual unit of the Bible is understood and proclaimed.

Preachers with a sense of the canonical narrative are ready to preach God, the one who empathically reconciles and redeems the world through Christ, from every text. Most every text contains the trouble of sin or the grace of God or both.[6] Those texts that contain only one, trouble or grace, or don't seem to contain "God" at all, rely on the rest of the canon for the fullness of the gospel. This is why it's imperative for the preacher to have some picture of the overarching biblical story like the one found below.

This graphic captures my sense of the narrative, though you might have a different take. I have used this picture to guide me in two ways. First, when my sermon is written I ask myself, which part of the biblical story does the text I'm preaching primarily tell? Is it more in line with trouble or grace, the problem of human sin or the resolution of God's love? Second, this graphic helps to provide from the biblical canon what my particular preaching text doesn't contain. If my text is void of trouble or grace, the biblical canon provides both.

THE BIBLICAL STORY

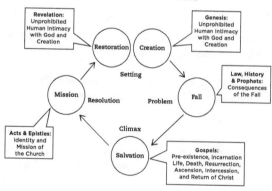

I don't always, or often, understand how the spirit of God works in the hearts of people through the preaching event. Who does? But I'm convinced that when God is the center of preaching, the hero and highpoint of the sermon, miracles happen. Callous people become empathic like God.

Preach as a Spiritual Discipline

Simon Baron-Cohen argues that "when you treat someone as an object, your empathy has been turned off."[7] Preachers are tempted to objectify the homiletic process, and maybe even the people to whom we preach. Modernity taught that the way to arrive at empirical truth is through detached objectivity. "Keep your subjective soul out of your epistemological quest for truth or you will skew the results." This notion, in the back of the preacher's mind, forces the preacher to separate her homiletical reading of scripture for the sermon from her devotional reading of scripture for the soul. Never the two shall meet. Detached objectivity over empathic sensitivity results in preachers who are more enamored with the preaching craft than the Christ who is preached and the people to whom he is proclaimed.

The practices that follow help preachers engage sermon preparation as a spiritual discipline. Preachers are not called simply to the task of getting a talk; we are summoned into a spiritual journey to get God. Most preachers just before delivery will, like a desperate quarterback with five seconds left in the football game, at least throw a homiletical Hail Mary, a quick "God, please bless the delivery and impact of this sermon." But we can do better.

Consider peppering the homiletic process with prayer before, during, and after the preaching event. Before you begin to craft the sermon, read a small portion of Psalm 119 imploring God to ignite your love for his word. During the day of the preaching event, do a prayer walk around the sanctuary inviting God's presence and power upon his people. After the sermon is delivered, journal an empathic prayer for the congregation based on the sermon's thrust. Abiding in God throughout the homiletic process is key to increasing the flow of empathy into the sermon and preaching event.

Start a Pre-Sermon Support Team

In *What Do They Hear: Bridging the Gap between Pulpit and Pew*, Mark Alan Powell exposes the ways that clergy and laity interpret the Bible differently based upon "empathy choices."[8] When reading a biblical narrative, clergy tend to identify with Jesus and/or the spiritual hero of the story. Powell calls this "idealistic empathy choices." Laypeople, on the other hand, relate mostly to the ignorance and mistakes of the disciples and/or the villain and victim of the story. Powell calls this "realistic empathy choices." These divergent empathy choices lead clergy and laity to identify with different characters and, thus, interpret the text from variant points of view. The result is an interpretive gap between pulpit and pew.

Wise preachers address this "gap" by finding ways to interpret scripture and develop sermons in conversation with the laity. Consider gathering ten to fifteen of your congregants in the middle of the week. This group should be diverse enough to represent a cross section of your congregation. You may want to form a new group every month or two so that all of your people will have the chance to participate over time.

Read and study the text together. Invite the group to offer observations, ask questions, and suggest interpretive possibilities. If the text is narrative in genre, ask the group to identify the character with whom they empathize most. Reflect with the group on ways the biblical text comforts, corrects, convicts, commends, or challenges.

I know of a pastor who preaches his "almost finished" sermon to the church elders every Tuesday at noon. The elders help him finish the sermon by offering questions and feedback on behalf of the congregation. This practice has the potential to heighten the preacher's understanding of and, therefore, empathy toward the people who hear the sermon.

Engage in Empathic Exegesis

In her book *Pray Without Ceasing: Revitalizing Pastoral Care*, Deborah Van Deusen Hunsinger writes, "The skills involved in listening to another with empathy are remarkably similar to those required in carefully reading a text."[9] Empathic biblical exegesis requires a hospitable openness in the interpreter, a willingness to be led where the text wants to go. Empathic exegesis is a lot like having a considerate conversation with a friend. We try to resist the urge to think about what we want to say in order to fully attend to what our friend is saying.

So, how can we read and interpret scripture empathically? For starters, try to empathize with not just the hero but the victim and the villain of a biblical narrative. Consider not just the perspective of the young stone-slinging David but the viewpoint of the sword-wielding Goliath or the power-hungry King Saul. When interpreting the struggle between Jesus and the scribes, try empathizing with those legalistic lawyers. Putting ourselves empathically in the sandals of the victim or villain, not just the hero, enables us to stretch our empathic muscles and preach the old familiar story in new and fresh ways.

Employing our imagination through the five senses is another way to enter into the biblical text. Ignatius of Loyola, a sixteenth-century Catholic priest, was the first to organize and popularize this merging of scripture and prayer with the imagination. Read a story from one of the four Gospels, or any narrative-genre text in the Bible. As you read, use your senses to empathically imagine your way into the scene. What do you see, smell, hear, feel, or taste? Consider what different characters in the story sense. As you do, you will experience empathic identification with the characters that enlivens preaching.[10]

Of course, our empathic imagination functions best in tandem with scholarly interpretation. Here, too, we can engage empathically by listening to the diversity of voices available to us in biblical scholarship. We need to hear from not only the "Lone Ranger," but the "Tantos"[11] who might offer a different interpretive angle than the one to which we are accustomed. Leonora Tubbs Tisdale rightly asserts that interaction with a "diversity (historic, geographic, ecclesial, racial, gender based, and socio-cultural) of theological dance partners in the interpretive process" brings into the light the preacher's and congregation's perspectives and preferences so they can be "illumined, examined, and challenged."[12]

An Asian Reformed Bible scholar in her seventies is going to consider interpretive angles on a text that an African American Methodist preacher in his thirties might overlook. The point is that reading the Bible empathically through the eyes of the "other" can unearth my personal biases and reveal fresh interpretive insight.

Consider Concentric Contexts

A sermon that faithfully expounds a biblical text in its literary and historical context but never grounds the exposition in the congregational context is really just a Bible study. Paul Scott Wilson's *The Four Pages of the Sermon* presents a thoughtful strategy for first locating God's action in the text and then connecting it to what God is doing in the congregational context. Preachers who empathically locate a corresponding plotline between the trouble and grace in the text and the trouble and grace in the context are well on their way to offering sermons that are "faithful and fitting."[13]

Considering concentric contexts transforms biblical exposition into sermonic expression. When I was preaching on a weekly basis, I devoted Monday and Tuesday to exegeting the biblical text, listening on behalf of my congregation for a "word from the Lord" from the word of the Lord. Once the sermon focus (some call it the "theme sentence," "main point," or "big idea") came into view, I prayerfully and empathically considered how the main thrust of the sermon intersected the various contemporary contexts of the preaching event.

I started close to home and then worked outward. First, I considered how the sermon focus confronted and/or comforted me. In other words, I engaged the text devotionally. I started to notice that the sermons I preached with the most power are the ones in which I wrestled personally and devotionally with the angle of the text. When that happened, I usually came away enthusiastically limping with Jacob under the weight of a word from the Lord.

Then, I considered how the "word" for the coming Sunday intersected the realities in our congregational life together. How does the sermon focus correct and/or confirm our theological convictions and communal practices? I tried to imagine how specific people might hear the trouble or grace in the sermon. Peter Jonker is spot on. In *Preaching in Pictures: Using Images for Sermons That Connect*, he writes, "Putting yourself in a specific listener's shoes can make certain parts of the text leap out at you, it can bring certain gracious promises to the surface; it can stimulate new questions."[14]

On the heels of that consideration, I reflected on how the sermon addressed the larger community around the church. I empathically asked, "Where is the gospel in this sermon for our community?"

There are national situations, struggles, and trends that can be probed through the lens of the sermon focus. How does this sermon focus offer hope for the hurting in our nation? How does this word from the Lord counter unexamined but harmful national trends?

Technology, immigration, and ease of travel have globalized us. What happens globally impacts us locally. A careful consideration of how the sermon connects to world concerns is warranted. What good, bad, or ugly global phenomenon is countered or confirmed by the gospel voiced through the coming sermon?

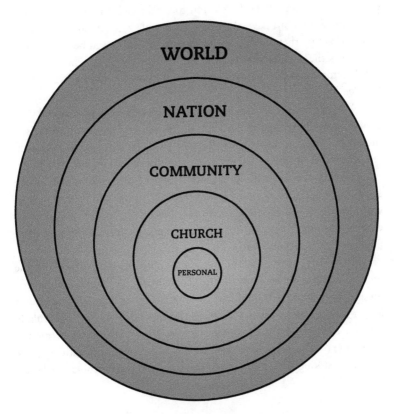

Usually on Wednesdays I allowed the sermon focus to wander empathically through my life, the congregation, the community, the nation, and the world. Most of the time, I found many points of contact between my exegesis of the text and my exegesis of the contexts. I came away with more sermon illustrations, implications, and applications than I could possibly use. I never had to run to those books promising fresh illustrations that thousands of preachers have already used. Considering concentric contexts turns a Bible study into a relevant sermon, putting contextual flesh on the exegetical bones.

Picture Your People

We've already noted in the previous chapter how pictures can induce empathy. At some point before you finish writing the sermon, pause to picture your people. Pray the sermon focus through the pictorial church directory. If you don't have pictures of the people who attend your church, you can picture them with your imaginative eye. Or, even better, you can bring back the pictorial directory! "A thumbing through the church's pictorial directory" can help pastors "summon to mind all manner of life's hard knocks."[15]

Work alphabetically through the directory of people who attend your church. Prayerfully imagine how specific people might respond to the sermon focus based on their particular situations. How might Joanne, a divorced mother of three small children, hear this sermon focus? How might Al, a seventy-year-old with lung cancer, connect with this word from the Lord? How might the sermon focus present good news to Erin, a sixteen-year-old whose parents are addicted to heroin? Simply work through the church directory in alphabetical order, praying for a dozen or so people and families each week you preach.

This thirty- to sixty-minute exercise, more than any other, did the most to increase my empathy for the people to whom I preached. I prayed for as many people as I could, but I wasn't in a hurry. I paused and prayed longer for those people who might find the impending sermon particularly difficult or hopeful. When I went back to finish writing the sermon, I made sure to edit out esoteric mumbo jumbo and replace it with language that earthed kingdom reality in the real lives of the real people to whom I preached.

Identify the Needs

As the preacher comes to empathically know and love the people in the preaching context, he or she will discern their specific needs. Paul Scott Wilson says, "Each time we preach we should try to identify some need in the congregation that our message seeks to meet."[16] The sermon should address felt and real needs.

Maslow's *Hierarchy of Needs* can be a helpful guide in detecting congregational needs that intersect your sermon. Maslow moves from basic human needs related to physiology and safety to higher-level needs of belonging, esteem, and self-actualization. It's crucial to consider these human needs more from a theological than a psychological or physiological basis, since the goal of Christian preaching is the reconciliation of God with humanity.

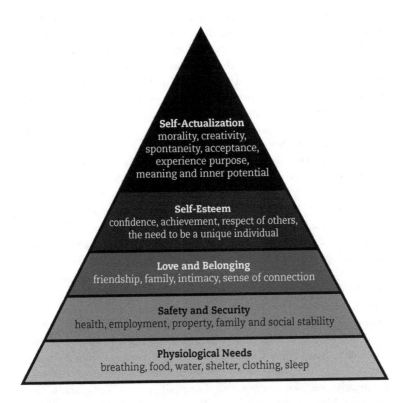

The next time you preach, try to identify two or three human needs that you sense God wants to address through the sermon. Spend some time throughout the week praying that listeners will be open to God's grace through the message. Pray that people will be joyfully surprised by the power of God to meet our deepest desires and "every need out of his riches in the glory that is found in Christ Jesus."[17] Empathically sensing what God might be "up to" in peoples' lives through the sermon while we preach it is cause for passionate preaching.

Connect with Diverse Listening Styles

We preach to congregations that are ethnically, generationally, economically, and educationally diverse. As if that weren't challenging enough, there is a diversity of listening styles too. The empathic preacher finds a way to put the gospel in a container from which a variety of listeners can drink.

Some people listen to sermons with their *mind* for exegetical information. No word study is too exhaustive and no historical background too detailed for them. These listeners want the preacher to go deep into the weeds of a single biblical text. They really do want to know what happened to the Jebusites. Sermons titled "Sources of Conflict in the Corinthian Congregation" or "Colossal Christological Claims in Colossians" (how's that for alliteration!) are music to their ears.

Others listen to the sermon with their *heart* for illustrative inspiration. They lean in when the preacher tells a humorous or emotional story. These are the only listeners in the congregation who want more personal anecdotes about the preacher's spouse and children. You might see them cry or hear them laugh. They want their heart moved with sermons titled something like "You Matter to God" and "God Comforts the Hurting."

There are those who listen to the sermon with their *soul* for theological reflection. They are more interested in the theological forest than the exegetical trees. Topical sermons that incorporate multiple passages dealing with the way and will of God excite them most. They refuse to accept simple answers to complex questions. Safe space to wrestle with God regarding the larger questions of life is what these listeners crave most. Sermons with titles like "Implications of the Incarnation" or "God and the Problem of Evil" appeal to them.

Finally, some listeners access the sermon with their *strength* for practical application. They might check out mentally when the preacher dives deep into the exegetical weeds or surveys the theological landscape. But when the preacher begins to explore what the embodiment of the Sunday sermon entails on Monday, they are all ears. They want to know how to apply their Christian faith at home, in the workplace, and at school. They are hands-on types who love sermons like "Principles of Holy Time Management" and "How to Have a Healthy Marriage."

You're probably wondering: How can I craft sermons that connect with such diverse listeners? First, know and counter your own listening preferences. We tend to preach most naturally to those whose listening style matches our own. So, if you tend to listen to sermons with your mind for information, for example, you will likely preach messages that are chock full of exegetical gems from the text. But, if you overplay your preferences you will abandon those who listen with their heart, soul, or strength. Admitting and, to an extent, abandoning your own preferences in order to reach a diversity of listeners is downright empathic.

Another way to connect with a diversity of listeners is to include in every sermon exegetical information for the mind, illustrative inspiration for the heart, theological reflection for the soul, and practical application for the hands. After you craft your sermon, go through and label each paragraph or section with "mind," "heart," "soul," or "strength/hands." This will enable you to see what to cut and what to add.

You could also employ a new sermon form to address listener diversity. "Love the Lord your God with all your heart, soul, mind, and strength," part of the *shema*, is the most often repeated command in the Bible and encompasses the four ways listeners tend to listen. Consider adding the shema sermon form to your homiletic mix. Structure your sermon with the following progression of movements:

- illustrative inspiration for the heart

- exegetical information for the mind

- theological reflection for the soul

- practical application for the hands

Watch people lean in when you speak their sermonic "love language."

Contemplate Various Vantage Points

The 2008 movie *Vantage Point*, starring Dennis Quaid and Forest Whitaker, is about an attempted assassination of an American president. The movie explores the scene of the crime from the vantage point of multiple people who experienced the event. Everyone sees something different based upon their location at the scene, their vantage point. When it comes to preaching, people hear the sermon differently based upon their life-situational point of view.

It is crucial for preachers to be aware of the multiple vantage points represented in the congregation when speaking about hot topics like sexuality, abortion, divorce, and politics. Will the rebellious teenager, sickly senior, jobless mid-lifer, divorcée, Latino, and widower respond to your assessment of the issue with a "yep," a "nope," or a "huh"? The ultimate aim of discerning where your people stand is not pandering but empathizing. I'm not advocating the compromising of biblical convictions, just the contextualizing of them.

Empathy demands both honesty and sensitivity. Preaching with empathy entails speaking to and for people on all sides of a given issue. The voice of the biblical witness has the place of primacy on any topic. We are called to preach "the whole truth and nothing but the truth so help us God."

However, like Christ according to John 1:14, our sermons must embody grace along with truth, without conceding either. Paul Scott Wilson, in *Preaching as Poetry: Beauty, Goodness, and Truth in Every Sermon*, describes how preachers can honor different viewpoints without abandoning biblical truth. The preacher must realize that "expectations of undue sameness can make some listeners feel invisible," but "in spite of differences, realistically a preacher finally has to land somewhere and invite people to act in faithful ways."[18] Grace *and* truth is the goal.

Empathically considering multiple vantage points enables the preacher to communicate with Christlike compassion and winsome grace. Sometimes we preachers proclaim hard, even painful truth in an unnecessarily arrogant, angry, or apathetic manner. These postures in the preacher are met with defensiveness in the listener. But if listeners on all sides of an issue feel as if you "get them," even if you disagree with their position, they are more likely to hear you and "get God." The goal of Christian proclamation is not rightness but reconciliation. I'm not suggesting that biblical truth doesn't matter. It does immensely. All I'm asking for here is that we share the hard truth with people much like a loving mother offers direction to her children.

I remember years ago hearing a popular evangelistic preacher speak to a massive crowd about abortion. Most of what he said was true. I agreed with his biblical perspective on the issue. He resonated with churchgoing folk, many of whom would never even consider having an abortion, let alone have had one. As far as I could tell, however, there was no redemptive grace offered along with the bold truth. If I were a woman who has had an abortion I would walk out, maybe even run out of the arena. Every woman I know who has had an abortion already feels a load of guilt and shame. None of them need coaxing into shame; they need grace to move on any regret that plagues them. Somehow the preacher's words must offer that vantage point too. Jesus "came from the Father full of grace and truth" (John 1:14 NIV). So must the preacher.

Prioritize Prepositions and Pronouns

Compelling preachers possess the authority of authenticity. To put it another way, they come across as one *among* not *above* the congregation. They don't diminish the importance of their prophetic role as a spokesperson for God. They speak with authority. Neither do they forget their priestly role as a spokesperson for humanity. They speak with authenticity.

Authentic preachers understand the prepositional directions of preaching. We don't only preach "to" or "at" people as prophets, but "with" and "for" them as priests. Holding these in tension keeps the preacher from falling off the extreme ends of dictating and pandering.

When we rightly order the prepositions that guide our preaching, the proper use of pronouns will follow. The level of empathy in preachers can be gauged by their use of pronouns. When I hear a preacher, male or female, speak to a mixed-gender crowd using "he" and "his" or "she" and "her" as exclusive generic pronouns, I cringe. Will the other gender in the room conclude that the sermon is not for them? Some of the most popular and celebrated preachers have yet to figure out a way to empathically employ gender-inclusive pronouns.

This may seem like a nitpicky splitting of politically correct hairs, but to me the gospel is at stake. Christ found a way to value and empower both Jew and Greek, slave and free, male and female. Sermonic language, if truly Christian, will do the same.

Another pronoun problem surfaces with the use of "us" and "we" versus "them" and "they." Of course there are appropriate times to use third-person pronouns, but not when, for example, we talk about the poor, divorced, ethnic minorities, and addicts who may be sitting there listening to the sermon. I've heard preachers berate "them" Democrats, wrongly assuming that only Republicans were in the congregation. I've heard Republicans referred to in similar ways. When our use of pronouns is more exclusive than inclusive, it's hard to preach the gospel with redemptive and reconciliatory power.

One final thought about the use of pronouns. Preachers debate whether or not to use "you" when challenging the congregation. It might be my generational preference, but as the culture still reels from the realities of postmodern repulsion for authority and attraction to authenticity, we should employ as often as possible first-person plural pronouns like "we" and "us" in place of the second-person use of "you." When I hear a preacher indict or command with "you," I bristle. "You need," "you must," "you ought," and "you should" make me want to stand up and say, "Who do you think you are, preacher?" And I'm a fairly friendly, laid-back kind of guy. Chances are, there are other Gen-Xers like me, not to mention Millennials, in your congregation who probably feel the same way.

Pepper with Contextual Colloquialisms

Leonora Tubbs Tisdale encourages preachers to employ "folk speech," which she defines as "the ordinary, everyday, language of local congregations." She adds, "The more the preacher can interpret Scripture and its symbols within the particular language of the congregational subculture...the more 'down to earth' the sermon will seem to a local community."[19] Preaching with empathy means speaking the language of *your* people.

I suppose that, to an extent, this is somewhat intuitive for preachers. But if we do intentionally what we've done intuitively, we can preach with greater empathy. An African American pastor in a black urban congregation can get away with the use of "ain't." A Caucasian pastor in an agricultural setting can get away with "fixin' to" do something. But the pastor of a suburban church in a university town may want to avoid using "ain't" and "fixin' to" and instead employ "epistemological" and "exacerbate" frequently. When I pastored a congregation that was essentially an addiction-recovery church, I could use terms like "copping" and "detox." Most everyone knew the meaning of those words.

Metaphors and images are colloquial too. Peter Jonker says, "If you want to find images that connect, you need to know the lives and stories of the people to whom you are preaching."[20] I heard an African American pastor preach a message on Joseph the dreamer from Genesis to a black urban congregation. He focused on how God can do better than our dreams. He said, "You dreamin' about a Lexus? God can do better than that. You dreamin' about a house in Roland Park? God can do better than that. You dreamin' about a degree from Compton? God can do better than that. You dreamin' of a gold chain around your neck? God can do better than that." The preacher knew his people well and spoke their language via the imagery, metaphor, and slang with which they could relate. These colloquialisms wouldn't connect with every congregation, but that's precisely how you know the sermon was empathically contextual. The more contextually colloquial the sermon, the less likely it can be preached in another setting without major adjustments.

Every context has its own brand of communal colloquialisms. Empathic connection to congregants will guide the preacher in the best use of terms, metaphors, and images that resonate. So go ahead and pepper your sermon with colloquialisms.

Deliver with Empathy

We learned about mirror neurons in chapter 2. They have a huge bearing upon empathy in sermon delivery. UCLA neurologist Marco Iacoboni writes that "mirror neurons fire when we see others expressing their emotions." Those neurons "help us understand the emotions of other people."[21] So when we look into the eyes and at the facial expressions of the people to whom we preach, it causes our mirror neurons to fire and give us a sense of what listeners are thinking and feeling. When we are attentive to listeners with our eyes while preaching, we adjust what we're saying and how we're saying it based on the nonverbal cues of listeners. Even Augustine in the fourth century taught preachers to make empathic adjustments in response to the nonverbal cues of listeners. He wrote to preachers that if you see a listener open his mouth "no longer to express approval, but to yawn," employ humor to get them back.[22]

Manuscript preaching has some advantages but can diminish the empathic connection between the preacher and listeners. Strong eye contact, almost intuitively, creates an empathic link. It seems worthwhile, then, for preachers to devote, at minimum, 25 percent of their overall sermon preparation time to the prayerful internalization and memorization of the manuscript. I suspect most of us were taught to embrace the importance of maintaining eye contact while preaching because of its rhetorical appeal. I'm asserting that eye contact is crucial because of its empathic stimulus. The "in-the-moment" preacher is able to see people and, immediately, preach with empathy.

Preach in Teams

One of the best ways to cast a larger empathic net in preaching is to utilize a preaching team. This can be done in any size congregation by empowering staff and/or lay preachers. I discovered the power of a preaching team by accident. We launched a Saturday service in a congregation I served as lead pastor. I was preaching every Saturday evening and twice on Sunday morning. Frankly, exhaustion forced me to recruit others to help me preach.

I began to preach two or three times monthly, while pastoral staff preached the other weekends. Our care pastor found a tight empathic bond with longtime churchgoers, especially seniors, when she preached. She knew them and they trusted her. Our outreach pastor connected extremely well with people in the recovery community and new believers when he preached. Of course, young families and teenagers enjoyed the empathic vibe with our family life pastor when he preached.

Every preacher connects more naturally with some listeners than others. Preaching in teams allows more voices to speak into the hurts and hopes, disappointments and dreams of a wider swath of people in your church. This doesn't let us off the hook, though. We still need to stretch our empathic reach beyond our natural affinities if we're going to preach better sermons and make better disciples.

Lead a Post-Sermon Discussion Group

Here's a way to knock out two birds, homiletic and discipleship, with one stone. Lead a discussion group about the content of the sermon after it's delivered. You can make this an open group or handpick ten to fifteen of your laypeople to participate. Perhaps you can invite this same group to serve also as your pre-sermon support team discussed earlier. The first hour of your midweek meeting can focus on feedback regarding the previous Sunday's sermon, while the second hour might attend to input for the upcoming Sunday sermon. Empathic preachers invite the people to whom they preach to inform and evaluate their preaching. Input and feedback is a prerequisite for preaching with empathy.

There are numerous possible questions for the post-sermon discussion group (PSDG). The sky's the limit, really. You'll want to ask questions that help you probe the discipleship and preaching needs of your congregants. The following inquiries can get you started:

- How did God speak into the particularities of your life through the sermon?

- At what point in the sermon did you most encounter God?

- What about the sermon elicited agreement, disagreement, or confusion?

- What did you learn about the Bible that you didn't know already?

- What did the sermon reveal about God?

- In what ways did the sermon confirm or challenge your thoughts, words, and/or behaviors?

Constructive, honest, and specific feedback can help preachers reach their empathic preaching potential. These penetrating questions not only will yield feedback about your preaching, but will lead your people away from the shallows and into the depths of the discipleship pool. As you rotate new people into the PSDG, you will come to know your people and their preaching needs more intimately.

Survey the Whole Flock

The pre-sermon support team and post-sermon discussion group will offer input and feedback, respectively, on a rather small scale and over a long period of time. One of the best ways to gather large-scale data quickly is through a Sunday service survey. Congregants should be able to complete the survey in three to five minutes during the service. Perhaps you can invite them to complete it during the offering. You might also consider doing two surveys on consecutive Sundays, one to solicit informative input and the other to invite evaluative feedback.

Your survey should seek input from the congregation that will inform future preaching. Make the survey anonymous but gather some basic demographic information. The survey should gauge what life topics, Christian doctrines, and biblical books are of interest to the congregation. You may want someone who loves to crunch information to tabulate the data for you. Here is a sample survey to solicit input for preaching.

SURVEY OF THE CONGREGATION

Your spiritual needs matter to us because you matter to us.
Please take a moment to express your sermon interests and needs by completing this survey and placing it in the offering plate later in the service.
Number of years as a follower of Christ: _____
Number of years at this church: _____
Your age: 16-25, 26-35, 36-45, 46-55, 56-65, 66-75, 75+

Topics
Please circle three topics which you would like to see addressed in an upcoming sermon or sermon series.

addiction	finances	leadership	sexuality
compassion	forgiveness	marriage	suffering
courage	friendship	parenting	temptation
dating	God's will	politics	use of time
depression	humility	racism	war
divorce	joy	servanthood	work

Doctrines
Please circle three Christian doctrines you would like to see addressed in an upcoming sermon or sermon series.

creation	sacraments (Baptism/Communion)
God, the Father	scripture
God, the Holy Spirit	sin
God, the Son	spiritual gifts
grace	The Church
heaven	The Incarnation
hell	The Second Coming
holiness	The Trinity
prayer	

Books of the Bible
Please circle three books of the Bible that you would like to see addressed in an upcoming sermon or sermon series.

Genesis	Job	Habakkuk	1 Thessalonians
Exodus	Psalms	Zephaniah	2 Thessalonians
Leviticus	Proverbs	Haggai	1 Timothy
Numbers	Ecclesiastes	Zechariah	2 Timothy
Deuteronomy	Song of Songs	Malachi	Titus
Joshua	Isaiah	Matthew	Philemon
Judges	Jeremiah	Mark	Hebrews
Ruth	Lamentations	Luke	James
1 Samuel	Ezekiel	John	1 Peter
2 Samuel	Daniel	Acts	2 Peter
1 Kings	Hosea	Romans	1 John
2 Kings	Joel	1 Corinthians	2 John
1 Chronicles	Amos	2 Corinthians	3 John
2 Chronicles	Obadiah	Galatians	Jude
Ezra	Jonah	Ephesians	Revelation
Nehemiah	Micah	Philippians	
Esther	Nahum	Colossians	

Other suggestions
Please list any other sermon topics you would like to see addressed:
_____.

Thanks for taking the time to complete this survey and for showing up hungry to worship and encounter God through the weekly sermon and other parts of the service.

Your other all-church survey should invite evaluative feedback about the preaching in your church. Again, you can give both surveys on the same Sunday or one each for two weeks. When soliciting evaluative feedback from the congregation about your preaching, be ready for critique. The sermons we preach are a part of us. They have our DNA all over them, assuming we're not downloading and preaching others' sermons. None of us like to hear that the sermonic babies we deliver are not as cute as we had hoped. In the long-run, though, both critique and commendation can be constructive.

The questions on the evaluative survey should be open-ended and limited to three or four. Here are some inquiries to consider posing to your flock: What do you appreciate most about the preaching in this church? What is one thing you would change about the preaching in this church? What recent sermon had a positive influence on your relationships with Christ and others? What other feedback can you give us to improve the preaching in this church?

Again, make sure you brace yourself for the affirmational and critical feedback you'll probably receive. Then, make the most of it as you empathically respond to your peoples' evaluation.

Reflect and Recover

Many preachers struggle with shame on the heels of the preaching event. Some call this the "Monday Morning Blues" (MMBs). The MMBs result from the voices in our heads that whisper shame into our ears. "You shouldn't have said that, you idiot. You should have said this but forgot, pea brain. You are not as good of a preacher as the one down the road or on your staff. You spent all that time preparing and nobody listened to a word you said. You'd be better off hanging up the homiletic cleats and calling it quits. Go sell cars." Even the most seasoned preachers among us experience shaming thoughts like these every now and then.

When preachers are overwhelmed by shame, they can't express the fullness of empathy toward others. Let's face it, preachers are notoriously self-critical and, thus, self-shaming. The good news is that while empathy can be stifled by shame, it can also annihilate shame. Brené Brown, in *Daring Greatly*, notes that self-empathy is a key to overcoming shame. "Self-compassion is key because when we are able to be gentle with ourselves in the midst of shame, we're more likely to reach out, connect, and experience empathy."[24] When you find yourself struggling with the shame of the MMBs or any other shame-inducer, show yourself some love. Immerse yourself in the empathy of God and others.

When I was preaching as a local church pastor, I did several things to reflect on and recover from the MMBs. First, after the Sunday sermon was delivered, I found a quiet location in the church to pray. I said to God something like, "I wish I hadn't said that" or "I wish I had said this." Basically, I voiced to God my regrets and feelings of shame. In ways I don't fully comprehend, God's empathic love washed most of the shame off of me in those moments. He spoke into my soul, "Well done, good and faithful servant" and "You are my beloved son with whom I am well pleased."

As I embraced God's empathy, I was able to express self-empathy. I worked on Mondays, but did low-stress and enjoyable tasks. I was easy on me. I ordered books to help me with an upcoming sermon series and cleaned my desk. I wrote notes or sent e-mails to encourage new believers or to appreciate volunteers. I typically scheduled a brunch with staff who energized me or new believers who excited me. At around 2 p.m., I would cut out from the office and go fly-fishing for trout at a local stream until dinner. In the evening, I would let my three small children jump all over me. When they got older, and too big to jump on me, we played board games or threw the football around. I did not meet with "extra grace required," hyper-critical types on Mondays. I was trying to recover from shame, not add to it.

Self-empathy as a tool for recovery from shame may seem selfish, but that couldn't be further from the truth. If shame blocks our capacity to express and preach with empathy, we had better deal with it. And self-empathy is "the real antidote to shame."[25]

Conclusion: Precision and Transformation

The contextual precision required for transformational preaching is born of empathic love. As you engage your heart, soul, mind, and strength in the practical exercises described in this chapter and the previous one, you will discover the power of preaching with empathy in a callous culture. There is no need to try all of these practices at once. Experiment with a few each week until you've experimented with all of them. Then stick with the ones you believe will increase your empathy most.

Conclusion

Back in chapter 2, I mentioned how a bishop sent one of my friends to serve a congregation, and the assignment seemed like a terrible mismatch. This pastor, an African American woman in her thirties, was appointed to a rural congregation in Iowa full of Caucasian farming families. You might expect an incompatible pairing like this to go south, and fast. But it didn't. Here is what the pastor recalled in her words to me:

> I tried to read magazines that reflected their mind-set, politics, and life-style as a way to understand them. I also made lots of home visits, more than five per week, in addition to my regular hospital and nursing home calls. Home visits with this group may have been around a quilt frame, in a kitchen during noodle making or jelly time, in the barn or cow pasture during chores, or a more traditional living room visit with tea and fresh cookies. Without these, I never could have understood how to connect this congregation to God through the sermon.

She learned that many of her church members considered themselves a part of bluegrass culture. Together, they began to weave bluegrass music into weekly worship. Members brought their accordions, banjos, and mouth harps to church. She said that, over a period of time, "I found my preaching adapting to the ways that they listened and, together, we met God in glorious ways!" People in the community heard that "the new preacher understood who they were." In less than a year, attendance at this rural congregation literally doubled from 60 to 120.[1]

Too many of my preaching colleagues and students suffer under a yoke of sermonic oppression that they need not bear. Admittedly, the preaching life is hard no matter how one lives it. Preaching is rigorous; but the joy is greater and the tenure longer when we practice preaching as a spiritual, contextual, intuitive, and creative art as opposed to a purely rhetorical, generic, detached, and mechanical science. Something happens to and through preachers who empathically bond with God and humanity. They begin to experience the process of developing and delivering sermons with joy, delight, surprise, energy, and freedom. Preaching with empathy makes what we preachers do so worth doing.

Notes

Introduction

1. Leonora Tubbs Tisdale, *Preaching as Local Theology and Folk Art* (Minneapolis: Augsburg Fortress, 1997), 23.

2. Simon Baron-Cohen, *The Science of Empathy: On Empathy and the Origins of Cruelty* (New York: Basic Books, 2012), 157.

1. A Culture of Apathy

1. Bibb Latane and John M. Darley, "Bystander Apathy," *American Scientist* 57, no. 2 (1969), 244.

2. John M. Darley and C. Daniel Batson, "From Jerusalem to Jericho: A Study of Situational and Dispositional Variables in Helping Behavior," *Journal of Personality and Social Psychology* 27, no. 1 (1973), 107.

3. Ibid., 107.

4. Barack Obama, "Commencement Speech," Northwestern University (June 19, 2006), accessed on November 13, 2017, http://www.northwestern.edu/newscenter/stories/2006/06/barack.html.

5. Diane Swanbrow, "Empathy: College Students Don't Have as Much as They Used To," Michigan News: University of Michigan (May 27, 2010), accessed on October 25, 2017, http://ns.umich.edu/new/releases/7724-empathy-college-students-don-t-have-as-much-as-they-used-to.

6. Christian Smith with Patricia Snell, *Souls in Transition: The Religious and Spiritual Lives of Emerging Adults* (New York: Oxford University Press, 2009), 68.

7. Ibid., 72.

8. I have corroborated the results of three different surveys. The findings from each survey reveal that the majority of pastors spend ten to fifteen hours each week in sermon preparation. Both Internet sources were accessed November 10, 2017. In a 2012 survey, 1,066 Southern Baptist pastors participated: http://www.lifeway.com/pastors/2015/06/08/pastors-and-time-in-sermon-preparation/. Thom Rainer conducted a Twitter poll in 2013 and the data can be found here: http://thomrainer.com/2013/06/how-much-time-do-pastors-spend-preparing-a-sermon/. Lori J. Carrell surveyed 482 Protestant pastors who spent eleven hours on average in sermon preparation. See *The Great American Sermon Survey* (Wheaton, IL: Mainstay Church Resources, 2000), 138.

9. Lori J. Carrell, *Preaching That Matters: Reflective Practices for Transforming Sermons* (Herndon, VA: The Alban Institute, 2013), 3.

10. David J. Lose, *Preaching at the Crossroads: How the World and Our Preaching Is Changing* (Minneapolis: Fortress Press, 2013), 7. Lose provides an excellent treatment of the challenges and opportunities of preaching in a postmodern world. See also David J. Lose, *Confessing Jesus Christ: Preaching in a Postmodern World* (Grand Rapids: Eerdmans, 2003).

11. Roman Krznaric, *Empathy: Why It Matters and How to Get It* (New York: Perigree, 2014), xxvi–xxvii.

12. Deism was a philosophy that emerged in Europe during the seventeenth century. Deists believe that while God created the world, God does not interact with the world.

13. Marshall B. Rosenberg, *Nonviolent Communication: A Language of Life* (Encinitas, CA: PuddleDancer Press, 2003), 129–39. Kristin Neff has built upon Rosenberg's work with the creation of a self-compassion scale.

14. Brené Brown makes this case in *Daring Greatly* (New York: Avery, 2012).

15. Krznaric, *Empathy,* 44–45.

16. Ibid., 160.

17. Ibid., 158.

18. Ibid.

19. James M. Lindsay, "The New Apathy: How an Uninterested Public Is Reshaping Foreign Policy," *Foreign Affairs* 79, no. 5 (September/October 2000), 7.

2. A Case for Homiletic Empathy

1. Derek Matravers, "Empathy as a Route to Knowledge," in *Empathy: Philosophical and Psychological Perspectives,* eds. Amy Coplan and Peter Goldie (Oxford: Oxford University Press, 2011), 19.

2. Amy Coplan and Peter Goldie, "Introduction," in *Empathy: Philosophical and Psychological Perspectives,* xxi.

3. Alvin I. Goldman, "Two Routes to Empathy: Insights from Cognitive Neuroscience," in *Empathy: Philosophical and Psychological Perspectives,* 32.

4. Roman Krznaric, *Empathy: Why It Matters and How to Get It* (New York: Perigree, 2014), x.

5. Ibid., 2.

6. Athanasius of Alexandria, *On the Incarnation.*

7. Krznaric, *Empathy,* 3–7.

8. Marco Iacoboni, *Mirroring People: The Science of Empathy and How We Connect with Others* (New York: Picador, 2009), 268.

9. Ibid., 7.

10. Ibid., 5.

11. Karen E. Gerdes, Elizabeth A Segal, Kelly F. Jackson, and Jennifer L. Mullins, "Teaching Empathy: A Framework Rooted in Social Cognitive Neuroscience and Social Justice," *Journal of Social Work Education* 47, no. 1 (2011), 113. The authors are citing the work of Schwartz and Begley from *The Mind and the Brain: Neuroplasticity and the Power of Mental Force* (New York: Harper, 2003).

12. Simon Baron-Cohen, *Zero Degrees of Empathy: A New Theory of Human Cruelty* (London: Allen Lane, 2011), 87, 118.

13. Karen E. Gerdes, et al., "Teaching Empathy," 113.

14. Lori Carrell, *The Great American Sermon Survey* (Wheaton: Mainstay Church Resources, 2000), 109.

15. Ibid., 95–100.

16. Lori Carrell, *Preaching That Matters: Reflective Practices for Transforming Sermons* (Herndon, VA: The Alban Institute, 2013), 183.

17. Ibid.

3. Empathic God

1. Marcel Sarot, "Divine Suffering: Continuity and Discontinuity with the Tradition," *Anglican Theological Review* 78 no. 2 (Spring 1996): 225. Sarot offers a rationale for and against both the *impassibility* and the *passibility* of God. In the end, Sarot asserts that divine *passibility* is the position closely in alignment with the God of the Bible and, therefore, worthy of embrace.

2. Jurgen Moltmann, *The Crucified God* (Minneapolis: Fortress Press, 1993), 248. "God is unconditional love, because he takes on himself grief at the contradiction in men and does not angrily suppress this contradiction. God allows himself to be forced out. God suffers, God allows himself to be crucified and is crucified, and in this consummates his unconditional love which is so full of hope."

3. Sarot, "Divine Suffering," 225.

4. Rob Lister, a prominent divine *impassibilist*, admits there is no biblical support for his position. He writes, "One cannot read Scripture and come away with the conclusion that God is affectionless." See Rob Lister, *God Is Impassible and Impassioned: Toward a Theology of Divine Emotion* (Wheaton: Crossway, 2013), 195.

5. Jennifer S. Croft and Alice Pyke, "Religious Diversity, Empathy, and God Images: Perspectives from the Psychology of Religion Shaping a Study Among Adolescents in the UK," *Journal of Beliefs and Values*, Volume 33, 2012 issue 3, 293–307.

6. Edward Farley, *Divine Empathy: A Theology of God* (Minneapolis: Fortress Press, 1996), 37.

7. Martin L. Hoffman, *Empathy and Moral Development: Implications for Caring and Justice* (Cambridge: Cambridge University Press, 2000), 3.

8. Moltmann, *The Crucified God*, 230. Moltmann uses the phrase "the suffering of love" to suggest God's voluntary willingness to be "affected by another."

9. Ibid., 222.

10. Catherine Mowry LaCugna, *God for Us* (San Francisco: HarperCollins, 1991), 272.

11. John Jefferson Davis, "What Is Perichoresis and Why Does It Matter? Perichoresis as Properly Basic to the Christian Faith," *Evangelical Review of Theology* no. 2 (2015): 146.

12. Moltmann, *The Crucified God*, 243.

13. Davis, "What Is Perichoresis and Why Does It Matter?", 147.

14. Wolfhart Pannenberg, *Systematic Theology*, trans. Geoffrey Bromiley (Grand Rapids: Eerdmans, 1991), 1:426.

15. Farley, *Divine Empathy*, 282.

16. Margaret Wise Brown, *The Runaway Bunny* (New York: HarperCollins, 1942).

17. See E. Ann Kaplan, "Empathy and Trauma Culture: Imaging Catastrophe," in Amy Coplan and Peter Goldie, eds., *Empathy: Philosophical and Psychological Perspectives* (Oxford: Oxford University Press, 2011), 257. Kaplan describes "empathic witnessing" as being moved to act on behalf of the person or group who is suffering.

18. See also Hebrews 2:5-18, which highlights Jesus's empathic connection to humanity.

19. Farley, *Divine Empathy*, 277–78. Here Farley argues that the empathy of Jesus "was not a private or interior phenomenon" but expressed itself through "public activity," including preaching.

20. Davis, "What Is Perichoresis and Why Does It Matter?" 155.

21. See Davis, "What Is Perichoresis and Why Does It Matter?" 156, and Stephen Seamands,

Ministry in the Image of God: The Trinitarian Shape of Ministry (Downer's Grove: InterVarsity Press, 2005), 148–49.

22. See Mark A. Maddix, "Unite the Pair so Long Divided: Justice and Empathy in Moral Development Theory," *Christian Education Journal*, no. 3, (Spring 2011): 59. Maddix makes the case that "as congregants engage in means of grace they become more empathetic and loving toward God and neighbor."

23. Dale P. Andrews argues for this in "African American Apprenticeship" in *The New Interpreter's Handbook on Preaching* (Nashville: Abingdon Press, 2008).

24. "Daniel Day-Lewis Aims for Perfection," *The Daily Telegraph* (London), February 2008, http://www.telegraph.co.uk/news/uknews/1579473/Daniel-Day-Lewis-aims-for-perfection.html.

25. Dietrich Bonhoeffer, *Life Together: The Classic Exploration of Christian Community* (New York: Harper & Row, 1954), 99.

4. Exemplars of Empathic Preaching

1. John Behr. Forward by C. S. Lewis. *On the Incarnation: Saint Athanasius* (New York: St. Vladimir's Seminary Press, 2012).

2. Hughes Oliphant Old, *The Reading and Preaching of the Scriptures in the Worship of the Christian Church: Moderatism, Pietism, and Awakening*, vol. 5 (Grand Rapids: Eerdmans, 2004), 110.

3. Ibid., 111.

4. John Wesley, Journal Entry March 29, 1739, in *The Works of John Wesley*, vol. 19, ed. W. Reginald Ward, Bicentennial ed. (Nashville: Abingdon, 1991), 46. Hereafter Wesley.

5. John Wesley engaged in field-preaching from 1739 to 1790, from the age of 35 to age 87.

6. Wesley, Journal Entry April 2, 1739.

7. Wesley used this phrase in his sermon "On Laying the Foundation of the New Chapel."

8. John Wesley, "A Farther Appeal to Men of Reason and Religion," in *The Works of John Wesley*, vol. 11, ed. Gerald R. Cragg (Oxford: Clarendon Press, 1975), 305–09. Hereafter Works.

9. Ibid., 306.

10. Richard P. Heitzenrater, "The Imitatio Christi and the Great Commandment: Virtue and Obligation in Wesley's Ministry with the Poor," in M. Douglas Meeks, ed. *The Portion of the Poor: Good News to the Poor in the Wesleyan Tradition* (Nashville: Kingswood Books, 1995), 63.

11. Works, "A Farther Appeal to Men of Reason and Religion," 306–07.

12. O. C. Edwards Jr., *A History of Preaching* (Nashville: Abingdon Press, 2004), 444.

13. Wesley, Journal Entry June 24, 1759, 203.

14. John Hampson, *Memoirs of the Late Rev. John Wesley, A.M.*, vol. 3 (Oxford: Sunderland, 1791), 158.

15. Wesley, Preface to Sermons, vol. 1, ed. Albert C. Outler, 104.

16. Old, *The Reading and Preaching of the Scriptures in the Worship of the Christian Church*, 115. This is from Wesley's *Standard Sermons*, 1:29.

17. In a letter written to John Chute on October 10, 1766. *Horace Walpole's Correspondence with John Chute*, et al., ed. W. S. Lewis et al., *The Yale Edition of Horace Walpole's Correspondence*, vol. 35 (New Haven: Yale University Press, 1973), 118–19.

18. This is from H. J. C. Grierson, ed., *Letters of Sir Walter Scott V* (Constable, 1933), 340ff. Found in *Henry D. Rack, Reasonable Enthusiast: John Wesley and the Rise of Methodism* (London: Epworth Press, 2002), 344.

19. Richard P. Heitzenrater, "John Wesley's Principles and Practice of Preaching," *Methodist History* 37, no. 2 (January 1999), 102–03.

20. Wesley, *Minutes of the Methodist Conference*, vol. 10, ed. Henry D. Rack, 859.

21. This is from John Wesley's *Directions Concerning Pronunciation and Gesture*.

22. Richard P. Heitzenrater, "John Wesley's Principles and Practice of Preaching," *Methodist History* 37, no. 2 (January, 1999), 102–03.

23. Vicki Tolar Burton, *Spiritual Literacy in John Wesley's Methodism: Reading, Writing, and Speaking to Believe* (Waco, TX: Baylor University Press, 2008), 31.

24. William H. Willimon and Richard Lischer, eds., *Concise Encyclopedia of Preaching* (Louisville, KY: Westminster John Knox Press, 1995), 288.

25. Richard Lischer, *The Preacher King: Martin Luther King Jr. and the Word That Moved America* (Oxford: Oxford University Press, 1995), 108–13. Lischer challenges the duplicity theory of Keith Miller.

26. "Man of the Year: Never Again Where He Was," *Time*, January 3, 1964, 14.

27. Richard Lischer, "Martin Luther King Jr.'s Preaching as a Resource for Preachers," *Journal for Preachers*, Easter 2000, 19.

28. Lischer, *The Preacher King*, 142.

29. Lischer, *Journal for Preachers*, 21.

30. See Martin Luther King Jr., "The Prodigal Son" in Mervyn A. Warren's, *King Came Preaching: The Pulpit Power of Dr. Martin Luther King Jr.* (Downer's Grove, IL: InterVarsity Press, 2001), 191ff.

31. https://kinginstitute.stanford.edu/king-papers/documents/i-have-dream-address-delivered-march-washington-jobs-and-freedom.

32. See Martin Luther King Jr. "A Christmas Sermon" delivered on Christmas Eve in 1967 at the Ebenezer Baptist Church. http://www.thekingcenter.org/archive/document/christmas-sermon#.

33. Martin Luther King Jr., *Antidotes for Fear, Strength to Love* (Minneapolis, MN, Fortress Press, 2010), 119-32.

34. Lischer, *The Preacher King*, 191.

35. Mervyn A. Warren, *King Came Preaching: The Pulpit Power of Dr. Martin Luther King Jr.* (Downer's Grove, IL: InterVarsity Press, 2001), 163. This is from a personal interview Warren had with Walter G. Muelder on March 4, 1966.

36. Lischer, *Journal for Preachers*, 19.

37. Paul Scott Wilson, *A Concise History of Preaching* (Nashville: Abingdon Press, 1992), 175.

38. Edwards Jr., *A History of Preaching*, 707.

39. Lischer, *The Preacher King*, 147.

40. Warren, *King Came Preaching*, 70.

41. Ibid., 27.

42. Lischer, *Journal for Preachers*, 20.

43. Lischer, *The Preacher King*, 170.

44. Lischer, *Journal for Preachers*, 20.

45. *Theological anthropology* formed part of the foundation for Wesley's high view of human capacity and restoration, especially compared to the Reformed thought of the day. This view was especially articulated in his sermon "Free Grace."

46. Richard Wayne Wills Sr., *Martin Luther King Jr. and the Image of God* (Oxford: Oxford University Press, 2009), 126–32.

47. See King, "Love, Law and Civil Disobedience," November 16, 1961, in *A Testament of Hope*, 48.

48. Rack, *Reasonable Enthusiast*, 343.

49. Willimon and Lischer, *Concise Encyclopedia of Preaching*, 289; Wilson, *A Concise History of Preaching*, 174.

50. Works, *A Farther Appeal to Men of Reason and Religion*, 397.

51. From King's sermon "The Three Dimensions of a Complete Life" delivered at the New Covenant Baptist Church in Chicago, on April 9, 1967.

5. Practices for Cultivating Empathy in Preachers

1. Roman Krznaric, *Empathy: Why It Matters and How to Get It* (New York: Perigree, 2014), 26; Simon Baron-Cohen, *Zero Degrees of Empathy: A New Theory of Human Cruelty* (London: Allen Lane, 2011), 184. Baron-Cohen argues that "empathy can be learned."

2. Colossians 1:27b.

3. Brené Brown, *Daring Greatly* (New York: Avery, 2012), 2.

4. Krznaric, *Empathy*, 114.

5. See Mark DeYmaz and Bob Whitesel, *re:MIX: Transitioning Your Church to Living Color* (Nashville: Abingdon Press, 2016) and David A. Anderson, *Multicultural Ministry: Finding Your Church's Unique Rhythm* (Grand Rapids: Zondervan, 2004).

6. 1 Corinthians 9:22b.

7. Krznaric, *Empathy*, 15.

8. Ibid., 74–76.

9. Acts 17:28b.

10. Dominic McIver Lopes, "An Empathic Eye," in Amy Coplan and Peter Goldie, eds., *Empathy: Philosophical and Psychological Perspectives* (Oxford: Oxford University Press, 2011), 118–33.

11. Krznaric, *Empathy*, 62.

12. Matthew 5:44a.

13. Fred B. Craddock, *Preaching* (Nashville: Abingdon Press, 1985), 97.

14. Krznaric, *Empathy*, 91.

15. Jo Berry, "Disarming with Empathy," Ted Talks, https://www.youtube.com/watch?v=coljnvVH18o. Published June 3, 2013, and accessed November 14, 2017. This video features Jo Berry, who has worked for over ten years to resolve conflict around the world. Sixteen years after her father was killed by an IRA bomb, Jo first met with the man responsible, Pat Magee. Her preparedness to try to understand him opened a path to empathy that continues to develop. Their unusual relationship has been told in the BBC documentary *Facing the Enemy*, was featured in the film *Soldiers of Peace*, and inspired *The Bomb*, a play by Kevin Dyer. The founder of Building Bridges for Peace, Jo Berry advocates that empathy is the biggest weapon we have to end conflict. She has spoken over one hundred times with Pat Magee and works regularly in the UK and in areas of conflict including Lebanon and Rwanda.

16. http://empathylibrary.com/. Accessed November 14, 2017.

17. Lopes, "An Empathic Eye," 125.

18. Jim Hemphill, "Movies as Empathy Machines," Moviemaker.com, Winter 2017.

19. Ibid., 40.

20. http://empathylibrary.com/. Accessed November 15, 2017.

21. Leonora Tubbs Tisdale, *Preaching as Local Theology and Folk Art* (Minneapolis, MN: Augsburg Fortress, 1997), 58.

22. Lenny Luchetti, *Preaching Essentials: A Practical Guide* (Indianapolis, IN: Wesleyan Publishing House, 2012), 75–78.

23. Scott Hoezee, *Actuality: Real Life Stories for Sermons That Matter* (Nashville: Abingdon Press, 2014), 45–46.

24. Krznaric, *Empathy*, 106–7.

25. Ibid., 160.

26. Romans 12:15a, NIV.

27. 1 Corinthians 11:33b, NIV.

28. Mark A. Maddix, "Unite the Pair So Long Divided: Justice and Empathy in Moral Development Theory" (*Christian Education Journal* 8, no. 3 (Spring 2011), 61.

29. Christine D. Pohl, *Making Room: Recovering Hospitality as a Christian Tradition* (Grand Rapids: Eerdmans, 1999), 13.

30. Matthew 9:10; Mark 2:15; Luke 7:34.

31. Dan King, "5 Ways You Can Care for the Environment," April 6, 2015, http://www.patheos.com/blogs/thehighcalling/2015/04/global-care-activist-faith/. I listed three of their five practices for creation care. Accessed November 10, 2017.

6. Practices for Infusing Empathy in Preaching

1. Kathryn A. Flynn, "The Storm of the I: Cultivating Empathy through the Choice of a Single Word," in *The CEA Forum*, Winter/Spring 2007: 36.1.

2. Ibid.

3. Ibid.

4. Leonora Tubbs Tisdale, *Preaching as Local Theology and Folk Art* (Minneapolis: Augsburg Fortress, 1997), 121.

5. G. Lee Ramsey, *Care-full Preaching: From Sermon to Caring Community* (Eugene, OR: Wipf and Stock, 2012), 143.

6. See Paul Scott Wilson, *The Four Pages of the Sermon: A Guide to Biblical Preaching* (Nashville: Abingdon Press, 1999). Wilson guides preachers on the practice of crafting sermons that capture both the "ancient trouble" and "ancient grace" in the biblical story in order to connect to the trouble and grace in the contemporary context.

7. Simon Baron-Cohen, *Zero Degrees of Empathy: A New Theory of Human Cruelty* (London: Allen Lane, 2011), 11.

8. Mark Allen Powell, *What Do They Hear? Bridging the Gap between Pulpit and Pew* (Nashville: Abingdon Press, 2007), 29–64.

9. Deborah Van Deusen Hunsinger, *Pray Without Ceasing: Revitalizing Pastoral Care* (Grand Rapids: Eerdmans, 2006), 65.

10. See Paul Scott Wilson, *Preaching as Poetry: Beauty, Goodness, and Truth in Every Sermon* (Nashville: Abingdon Press, 2014), 116–18. Wilson insightfully explores the necessity of using the imagination in preaching.

11. Tisdale, *Preaching as Local Theology and Folk Art*, 98. Tisdale is quoting Catherine and Justo Gonzalez here.

12. Ibid., 98.

13. Tisdale's phrase to describe the importance of sermons being faithful to the biblical text and fitting for the local context.

14. Peter Jonker, *Preaching in Pictures: Using Images for Sermons That Connect* (Nashville: Abingdon, 2015), 93.

15. Scott Hoezee, *Actuality: Real Life Stories for Sermons That Matter* (Nashville: Abingdon Press, 2014), 96.

16. Wilson, *The Four Pages of the Sermon*, 48.

17. Philippians 4:19b.

18. Paul Scott Wilson, *Preaching as Poetry: Beauty, Goodness, and Truth in Every Sermon* (Nashville: Abingdon Press, 2014), 62.

19. Tisdale, *Preaching as Local Theology and Folk Art*, 127.

20. Jonker, *Preaching in Pictures*, 116.

21. Marco Iacoboni, *Mirroring People: The Science of Empathy and How We Connect with Others* (New York: Picador, 2009), 119.

22. Augustine, *De Cat. Rud.* 13:19 (CCL 46:142-43); trans. Canning, 100.

23. Powell, *What Do They Hear?* 105. Powell is even more extreme. He asks preachers to consider the question, "Do we spend as much time practicing a sermon as we do composing it?"

24. Brené Brown, *Daring Greatly* (New York: Avery, 2012), 75.

25. Ibid., 74.

Conclusion

1. Interview with Rev. Dr. Safiyah Fosua. November 13, 2017.